A Primer of Clinical Intersubjectivity

A Primer of Clinical Intersubjectivity

Joseph M. Natterson, M.D.
and
Raymond J. Friedman, M.D.

JASON ARONSON INC.
Northvale, New Jersey
London

Production Editor: Judith D. Cohen

This book was set in 12 point English Times by TechType of Upper Saddle River, New Jersey, and printed and bound by Haddon Craftsmen of Scranton, Pennsylvania.

Library of Congress Cataloging-in-Publication Data

Natterson, Joseph M., 1923–
    A primer of clinical intersubjectivity / by Joseph M. Natterson and Raymond J. Friedman.
       p. cm.
    Includes bibliographical references and index.
    ISBN 1-56821-446-4
    1. Psychotherapist and patient. 2. Intersubjectivity.
  I. Friedman, Raymond J., 1942– . II. Title.
    [DNLM: 1. Psychoanalytic Therapy. 2. Psychoanalytic Theory.
  3. Professional–Patient Relations. WM 460.6 N282p 1995]
  RC480.8.N38 1995
  616.89′14 — dc20
  DNLM/DLC
  for Library of Congress   94-43799

Manufactured in the United States of America. Jason Aronson Inc. offers books and cassettes. For information and catalog write to Jason Aronson Inc., 230 Livingston Street, Northvale, New Jersey 07647.

For Idell and Jan,

with loving thanks.

Contents

Introduction

A sea change is occurring in psychotherapy. Radically new conceptions of the nature of psychotherapy, its meanings and methods, are crowding into the field. The traditional, formulaic, positivistic ways of defining and teaching therapy no longer hold sway. In the past, therapy, when taught and conceptualized, was somehow abstracted or lifted out of its human context, ostensibly in order to establish the science of psychotherapy. This procrustean tendency is rapidly becoming feebler, as psychotherapy is being studied and conceptualized in its own human terms.

The role of the therapist is central to this powerful new wave of thinking. That the therapist is a participant observer has been routinely acknowledged for many years, but when the therapeutic process was examined, the emphasis usually was on the observer therapist, rather than the participant therapist.

The history of what is now the new trend in psychotherapy is complex and is, perhaps surprisingly, even older than the history of psychoanalysis. Philosophers have long known that transformations of consciousness are involved in the achievement of self and that involvement in human relationships is important for changes in consciousness. Hegel (1807) long ago specifically cited the crucial importance of intersubjectivity in the achievement of self, and of course his thinking had evolved in part from the work of distinguished predecessors.

Some now argue that Freud's great contribution was the creation of a science of subjectivity. Jonathan Lear (1990) argues this point quite impressively. Although Freud (1912) developed a one-person, drive-based theory of personality development and of therapy, his theoretical position was inconsistent from the outset. He acknowledged the therapist's emotional involvement, albeit reactive and inconstant, calling it countertransference. Also, he emphasized the importance of unconscious communication between patient and therapist.

The later contributions of Ferenczi (1988), who emphasized the intense subjective involvement of the therapist and who recommended *mutual analysis*, were extremely important for the changes that are now occurring. Although his work was very controversial, it was widely known in psychoanalytic circles and had a deep influence on many younger psychoanalysts.

Some years later, Franz Alexander, a student of

Ferenczi, and Thomas French (1946) offered the principle of the *corrective emotional experience,* which required a kind of tailor-made subjective attunement by the therapist to the patient's psychological needs. This principle obviously directly contradicted the classical psychoanalytic requirement of a unitary, consistently neutral, unvarying technical stance by the analyst.

Although Alexander's work was not accepted as a legitimate part of prevailing psychoanalytic dogma, his contributions helped spawn a multitude of new concepts and technical innovations. Another important psychoanalytic innovator of the same period as Alexander was Karen Horney (1939), who gave a powerful impetus to feminist and interpersonal perspectives in psychoanalysis and psychotherapy.

Today, mainstream psychoanalysis is aware of the intersubjective dimension. This awareness has been due to the efforts of numerous contributors who have slowly deconstructed the dominant mechanistic, one-person psychological model. This "movement" has not been organized, but its relentless progression to the doorstep of intersubjectivity has occurred through the work of the following individuals (an incomplete list to be sure): Winnicott (1947, 1951), Macalpine (1950), Waelder (1956), Isakower (1957–1963), Loewald (1960), Racker (1968), Searles (1975), G. Klein (1976), Sandler (1976), Schafer (1976, 1983), Lipton (1977a, 1977b), McLaughlin (1981), Gill (1982), Gill and Hoffman (1982), Poland (1986, 1988), and Jacobs (1991, 1993).

More than fifteen years ago, Heinz Kohut (1977) proposed a new psychoanalytic approach that he called *self psychology*. Its salient characteristic is its focus on self and the absolute necessity for the development of the self in relationship to another self or selves. Kohut referred to the necessary other self as a *self object*. And he studied the effect of the self object upon the self in need, that is the patient. The self does not develop without the other.

Intersubjectivity is an aspect of phenomenological philosophy and psychology. Through the thinkers just cited (and numerous others), intersubjectivity has become increasingly important for understanding psychotherapy. Psychotherapy basically is an experience of clinical intersubjectivity.

In this book we strive to bring to the reader the basic principles of clinical intersubjectivity in psychotherapy, as well as a range of examples from our practices of psychotherapy and psychoanalysis.

Our overall aim is to provide the psychotherapist with a working knowledge of intersubjective perspectives, with every confidence that such knowledge will enlarge the reader's therapeutic understanding and power.

The adoption of an intersubjective perspective does not require that a therapist repudiate Freudian, Kleinian, interpersonal, object relations, or self psychological theories of personality and therapy. However, intersubjective orientation will transform the way such theories are regarded and employed. For example, any such theoretical construct will be seen as possibly useful, but necessarily incomplete, insofar as its intersubjective frame or context is not articulated. Adherence to a favorite theory becomes more flexible, more contextualized and historicized, due to an intersubjective awareness.

An intersubjective orientation requires a continuous appreciation of the overriding importance of the interplay of the subjective lives of both participants in the therapeutic situation. This does not mean paying lip service to the therapist's subjective involvement. In this work we offer a unique emphasis on the therapist's subjectivity. At all times, the reactive and initiating aspects of the therapist's subjective experience become important. We discuss the many variations of these intersubjective events. We show how they are influencing the immediate situation and how they provide opportunities for future therapeutic development.

Beyond these clinically important aspects of intersubjectivity, another issue is ever present. Commitment to intersubjectivity ultimately implies commitment to the universe, nothing less. The therapist's consciousness of each individual's active immersion in the universe is the transforming essential of intersubjectivity. Intersubjectivity entails reciprocal causal relationships of all parts of the human universe with all other parts. All human events are co-created by the participants. Everyone changes, and is changed by, everyone else.

A therapist who is thus informed is appreciative of the immense power that inheres compressed in the detail. Such a therapist also understands the infinite complexity of even the tiniest detail of life. These kinds of awareness enable the therapist to develop and maintain an attitude of ambiguity. This attitude continues even when the therapist engages in thoughts and interventions that seem to imply completion.

Paradoxically, the intersubjective perspective, which,

as just described, might seem grandiose, in fact sensitizes the therapist to detail and nuance — and enhances appropriate humility in him or her.

Some express fear that an intersubjective orientation will distract the therapist or will entail excessive attention to his or her subjective experience, resulting in neglect of the patient. In fact, the reverse is the case: increased sensitivity to any part of the therapeutic relationship enhances appreciation of all parts. Psychological growth of either party — patient or therapist — eventuates in growth of the other. In linguistic terms the guiding principle is *both-and*, not *either-or*.

This book employs a question-and-answer format. We have found it quite congenial to our intersubjective orientation. It seems to establish a more intimate exchange between us, the authors, and between us and you, the readers. It suggests a dialogue and helps avoid lecturing. This format, obviously, is in the spirit of intersubjectivity.

One final and important point. Our title is *A Primer of Clinical Intersubjectivity*. We could have omitted the word "clinical," but we believe that accuracy requires its inclusion. A primer of intersubjectivity would indicate an authoritative set of statements of a philosophical nature. We, the authors, are not philosophers; we are clinicians. In this project we have attempted to employ those elements of intersubjectivity that enrich clinical practice and theory. The influence of intersubjectivity on clinical issues is growing rapidly, but at present is still in a rudimentary stage. In this, we consider our work as sophisticated as any other offering in the area of clinical intersubjectivity. At this point of development, we are all writing primers!

Intersubjectivity Defined

WHAT IS INTERSUBJECTIVITY?

Intersubjectivity designates the basic process of psychotherapy. The term emphasizes the idea that in the therapeutic situation two individuals co-create the relationship they live and talk about. Intersubjectivity is the overarching term that refers to the reciprocal influence of the conscious and unconscious subjectivities of two people in a relationship.

This vignette illustrates an intersubjective moment, just one of thousands that occur continuously in psychotherapy: (JMN) A 34-year-old Argentinean woman has been in nonintensive psychotherapy for one year. We established a warm, candid relationship very quickly, and it has persisted from that time. Although she is brilliant, speaks six languages, and has held executive positions in international financial firms, she has been unemployed since we first met and began therapy. It has been obvious to both of us that her unemployment is due to the effect of the economic recession on international markets. Her current earnings are minimal and are derived from giving language lessons.

The patient has very scant economic resources, and she avidly pursues any appropriate job opportunities. Her current work problem does not seem to arise from neurotic inhibition. In this same period she has felt frightened, angry, and depressed.

She desperately wants to marry and have children, but her relationships with men have not led to marriage. During this period, she has involved herself in a series of sexual relationships in which she feels in love with men who are not available to her either because they are married or are psychologically uninterested in a lasting relationship.

The patient recently expressed the view that these masochistic sexual relationships have intensified due to the psychological impact of her current unemployment and consequent impoverishment. I heard this remark with much inner pain and understanding. I thought about the severe poverty of my family during my childhood and of how this terrible problem reverberated through the psychological lives of all of us in my family. I additionally tried to focus on the specific impact of our family's shared anxiety and shame upon our sexuality. Of course, I could only survey the influence on my own sexual fantasies and behaviors. The prevalence of my masochistic fantasies and sadistic actions during that period felt closely connected to the direct psychological consequences of the economic realities, although I am aware of other contributing factors.

These early economic terrors have effects upon me that linger to this day. In some manner, I bring them to every human encounter. It seems to me that with this patient, for example, I have sought—from the outset—maternal reassurance that there will be food and shelter for me and the rest of the family.

She, on the other hand, perceives me as warm, generous, and loving. She always feels that she has a safe haven in my office. Unlike me, she comes from a financially secure, professional, middle-class family. Like me, however, she was one of multiple children, and she experienced feelings of privation, envy, and consequent guilt in relation to her siblings with respect to parental interest and attention.

She and I have engaged one another with interpenetrating similar but also differing needs. There is continuous stimulation of these needs and a reliving of them, with consequent progressive transformations of self-consciousness resulting from the therapeutic flux.

This complex intersubjective process is epitomized by the patient's recent recognition that the severe economic anxiety over the past two years has induced an increase in the masochistic tendencies in her intimate, sexual relationships. This significant insight has arisen in part from the psychological input of both the patient and me.

DO ALL PSYCHOTHERAPISTS WHO ARE INTERESTED IN INTERSUBJECTIVITY EMPLOY THE TERM IN THE SAME WAY?

The answer is yes and no. Psychotherapists who are seriously interested in intersubjectivity all agree upon the mutual, reciprocal, interactional influence of each party upon the other and upon the whole. However, beyond this point of commonality, cleavages among the intersubjectivists become apparent.

First, it should be emphasized that theorists from various schools of psychotherapy are now acknowledging that intersubjectivity is the correct designation for the basic psychological processes at work. But then divergent points of view emerge. Our special focus of interest is on the vital significance of the therapist's subjectivity that continuously operates in the therapeutic process. Because the salience of this dimension of intersubjectivity seems to be generally neglected, we have chosen in this volume to place particular emphasis on this factor.

Some other contributors do not recognize or acknowledge that the therapist's subjectivity plays a continuous role in shaping the therapeutic process. These others employ their subjectivity only to understand what is transpiring "within" the patient and/or to correct disharmonies, impasses, disjunctions, and other problems arising in the therapy.

Jacobs (1991, 1993), starting from a classical base, bravely ventures into a world he calls "the interplay of two psychologies" (1993, p. 7). He believes "the inner experiences of the analyst often provide a valuable pathway to understanding the inner experiences of the patient" (1993, p. 7). We firmly agree with these ideas, but believe that Jacobs has only crossed the Rubicon halfway. The remaining steps would include the idea that the analyst's subjectivity or his personal world view directly and continuously influences the patient's subjectivity and world view.

One of the central ideas we propose is that the therapist and the patient do not simply bring to the therapy two separate and very private lives, with the only result being that the therapist and the patient come to understand only the patient's private world. Rather, the two people understand and change each other during the process of co-creating the therapy. It is a fiction to assume that there is a completely individuated patient with a fully formed mind that lies waiting like some buried treasure for discovery by the separate, fully formed mind of the analyst. Instead, therapist and patient are continuously defining themselves and each other.

Many authors have drawn attention to the limitations of the concept of countertransference (Epstein and Feiner 1979, 1981, Tansey and Burke 1989, Wolstein 1983, 1988, 1994). Natterson (1991) and Aron (1991a, b, 1992) strongly emphasize the idea that the word *counter* in the term countertransference draws attention away from the analyst's initiating role. Aron (1991a) notes that analysts are, of course, always responding to transference pressures from their patients but he states, "The term countertransference, though, obscures the recognition that the analyst is often the initiator of the interactional sequences, and therefore, the term minimizes the impact of the analyst's behavior on the transference" (p. 33). Aron (1991a) demonstrates that an important task of the analyst is to "bring into awareness and articulate the patient's denied observations, repressed fantasies, and unformulated experiences of the analyst" (p. 36).

Stolorow and his associates (Atwood and Stolorow 1984, Stolorow et al. 1987, 1992, 1994) have linked their intersubjective perspective to self psychology. Stolorow and co-authors (1994) state, "It is my view that the theory of intersubjectivity provides a broad methodological and epistemological net within which self-psychology can creatively expand" (p. 38). They see intersubjective analysis as the detection of the conjunction or disjunction of the two subjectivities, thus enabling the therapist to become a more effective self-object. They do not offer a description in their clinical writings of how the therapist's subjectivity shapes the therapeutic field during non-problematic phases of therapy.

Benjamin (1988, 1992), in a series of writings, has grappled with the complexities of an intersubjective point of view. She (1992) notes that recognizing the parent as a subject

> is a developmental process that has barely begun to be explicated. How does a child develop into a person, who, as a parent, is able to recognize her or his own child? What are the cultural processes, the psychic landmarks, of such development? Where is the theory that tracks the development of the child's responsiveness, empathy, and concern, and not just the parents' sufficiency or failure? [p. 46]

Benjamin (1988) points out that in the mother–infant relationship the mother is not simply an "object" who meets the infant's basic needs. As the child develops, he or she comes to recognize mother as a separate subject with her own needs and desires. This often forgotten step is heralded by Benjamin (1988) as a major developmental element with profound implications for future relating. Her ideas carry us far beyond the impersonal notion of object constancy, which views the principal goal of early development as recognition of mother as a stable, separate object. Stern (1985), Lichtenberg (1983,1989), and Beebe and Lachman (1988a, 1988b) are infant researchers who are working out the developmental details of these crucial early intersubjective events.

Schwaber (1981, 1983) tightly links her version of intersubjectivity to her concept of empathy. She (1981) says that empathy

> is that mode of attunement which attempts to maximize a singular focus on the patient's subjective reality seeking all possibilities to ascertain it. Vigilantly guarding against the imposition of the analyst's point of view, the role of the analyst and of the surround, received and experienced by the patient, is recognized as intrinsic to that reality; the observer is a part of the field observed as a scientific modality, empathy employs our cognitive, perceptual as well as affective capacities. [p. 60]

We disagree with Schwaber. It is impossible to avoid "imposition of the analyst's point of view." In fact, we acknowledge and study the role of the therapist's subjectivity.

In contrast to Schwaber, such authors as Hoffman

(1983, 1991a,b, 1992) and Renik (1993a,b) explicitly emphasize the imposition of the analyst's subjectivity. Each of these authors offers a strong theory for the central, inescapable role of the analyst's subjectivity on the therapeutic process.

Hoffman (1991a) espouses what he calls a social constructivist paradigm, in which the two participants co-create the psychotherapeutic realities. Hoffman believes that his position eliminates neither the historical nor the intrapsychic perspectives. He says, for example, that the eagerness to reduce classical psychoanalytic theory's overemphasis on the individual dimension should not cause a swing to overemphasizing the relationship dimension, producing an isolation of each from the other. He writes that shifting to a social constructivist paradigm does not have to entail such a reversal. In fact, he adds, it necessitates a synthesis of the two different perspectives, attended by an appropriate redefinition of each, taking into consideration their interdependence.

Hoffman sees the intersubjective as meaning that two hierarchically organized psychological systems interact at all levels. He means that this involves interaction at various levels of psychological organization and consciousness. He further insists that in this model the intrapsychic and the interpersonal cannot be divorced.

Renik (1993a,b) explores the "irreducible" influence of the analyst's subjectivity. Renik states that the analyst can only gain insight into his own psychological inputs after he has unconsciously enacted them. Commenting on the analyst's subjectivity, Renik (1993b) states:

Instead of saying that it is *difficult* for an analyst to *maintain* a position in which his or her analytic objectivity focuses on a patient's inner reality, I would say that it is *impossible* for an analyst to be in that position *even for an instant*; since we are constantly acting in the analytic situation on the basis of personal motivations of which we cannot be aware until after the fact, our technique, listening included, is *inescapably* subjective. [p. 560].

According to Renik (1993b), there are four technical implications to accepting the analyst's ever-present subjectivity. First, the standard ideal that holds that countertransference enactments are to be avoided has to be dropped. Second, Renik contends that personal motivations that are unconscious and that are expressed by the analyst in action not only cannot be avoided, but in fact are essential to the analytic process. This permits authentic corrective emotional experiences. Third, acceptance of the analyst's subjectivity does not lead to a reduced therapeutic discipline. Fourth, Renik, agreeing explicitly with Hoffman, emphasizes that neither the analyst's nor the patient's interpretation of reality is authoritative.

We regard Racker (who worked in the 1950s) as having been an intersubjectivist without portfolio. Witness this statement by Racker (1968):

The first distortion of truth in the "myth of the analytic situation" is that it is an interaction between a sick person and a healthy one. The truth is that it is an interaction between two personalities in both of which the ego is under pressure from the id, the superego, and the external world; each personality has its internal and external dependencies,

anxieties and pathological defenses; each is also a child
with his internal parents; and each of the whole personalities—that of the analysand and that of the analyst—
responds to every event of the analytic situation. [p. 132]

In this rich, condensed statement, Racker indicates that
interpersonal, structural, drive, and object relations
theory all exist under the overarching concept of intersubjectivity.

HOW IS INTERSUBJECTIVITY
DISTINGUISHED FROM THE
INTERPERSONAL AND THE
INTRAPSYCHIC?

The psychological life of the individual is constituted
essentially by his internal and interpersonal experiences.
Intersubjectivity refers to the process whereby these zones
of experience operate in the therapeutic relationship.

The terms *intrapsychic* and *interpersonal* have traditionally been important elements in the vocabulary of
psychotherapy. In its best sense, intrapsychic designates
the inner experience of the person. But the term also
implies a separateness of the internal psychological experience, with associated intimations of distinct boundaries
and a completeness of the individual unto himself. These
latter connotations are incompatible with the intersubjective point of view, which assumes a continuous interpenetration of the psychological experience of related

individuals. In a similar way, the term *interpersonal* is useful when it denotes the powerful interplay of the psychological lives of two persons in a relationship. However, there was a tendency in the past by psychotherapists of the interpersonal school to accord therapeutic importance only to the discernible interactions of the patient and therapist—with primary attention to how the patient shaped and reacted in the interpersonal situations. This tendency resulted in a relative neglect of the internal, unconscious, and historical dimensions of the patient's therapeutic involvement, as well as relatively insufficient attention to the therapist's subjectivity.

The terms *intrapsychic* and *interpersonal* can be quite useful components of the psychotherapeutic lexicon, but they must be separated from their traditional theoretical underpinnings.

We offer the following clinical example to acquaint the reader with our view of an intersubjective therapeutic process. It demonstrates how the inner lives of patient and therapist have reciprocal influence on one another, responding to and creating the intersubjective situation.

(RJF) This session occurred during the latter part of the second year of treatment. The early phase of therapy was characterized by Zac's idealization of the analyst as a guiding, affirming, and empowering father who reduced his anxiety and gave him permission to succeed in work and marriage. Zac's needs for fathering resonated with the therapist's propensity to seek a reassuring father. The analyst tolerated Zac's idealization and steadfastly, when appropriate, interpreted Zac's reliance on him as a strong father. The analyst was able vicariously to rework his own needs and conflicts in this area and to enjoy, also vicariously, the presence of an idealized father.

As he lay on the couch, Zac said, "I can't seem to get all the parts of my life working at once." I felt flat as I heard this comment and wondered why it did not arouse my curiosity. I rationalized that I was still distracted by phone conversations that preceded this, the first hour of the day for me. I also consoled myself with the idea that I was experiencing the end of a cold that left me a bit sluggish.

Zac next launched into a tirade against his wife for her display of "childish" behavior during his conversation with his 11-year-old daughter (from a former marriage) the evening before. I continued to feel slowed and uninterested, but I was hopeful that I would recover. Zac proceeded to berate his wife, which usually he did with considerable energy and at some length. However, today he was brief, and when he said that he was "puzzled and pissed" to discover that she was still angry the next morning, I suddenly had the thought of "freeze-drying" my wife the upcoming Saturday morning. Later in the day I would reconstitute her, so that we could go out for the evening. By now I was affectively alert, and I became curious about both the aggressive, destructive quality of the freeze-drying and the accompanying high level of eroticism. Before I could analyze my fantasy, Zac announced that he was "brilliant in business yesterday, and that it was a breakthrough day."

In rapid succession, Zac reported a dream from last night in which "I just concluded a very successful deal and then someone put a handcuff on my wrist to lead me off to jail."

Zac remarked, without much conviction, that he supposed it was his father punishing him for his success. This was an interpretive theme we had been working on vigorously in recent months, but now there was no enthusiasm for this idea that had recently been so liberating for him in his business activities. He seemed emotionally flat and at a dead end. I had nothing in particular to say; and while Zac associated on for a bit, I took a moment to analyze the intense fantasy about my wife, which I suspected represented the first phase of an interpretive process that I hoped would result in a useful construction to Zac.

My plans called for me to write on Saturday, and I was eagerly anticipating doing so. I thought of my wife and pictured her disliking my absence during a day of leisure, just as I would have disliked her similar absence. By freeze-drying her, I magically took care of her discontent. I could then achieve my professional goal while not irritating my wife who, after she was reconstituted, would not even know time had passed. Thus she would be available socially and sexually for me, and I could have my cake and eat it too. Then I began to wonder if I was accomplishing what Zac could not allow himself, namely to enjoy a basically satisfactory relationship with his wife. Simultaneously I became aware that my fantasy carried powerful competitive feelings between us, and I thought for a moment that I should pursue the subject of competitiveness, which recently had become a new and touchy theme in our relationship. I fleetingly wondered if my fuzzy-headedness at the beginning of the hour was caused by my fear of the competitive themes that now were causing ripples of anxiety in me.

I wish I could say that I know I chose with some degree of precision not to interpret the competitive theme, but I cannot. All I can tell you is that I did choose to interpret in a different direction. Perhaps I was led by a picture of my Aunt Jean that emerged in my mind. She had been a beautiful woman who was at times the fantasy object of my adolescent lust. I associated her to Zac's Aunt Rose, who served him identically in adolescence. Both were displacements from our sexually seductive mothers. The mother connection seemed even stronger when I reflected on the session later. I came to believe that the aggression in my fantasy of freeze-drying my wife stemmed from my familiar experience of mixed rage and love for my mother. I then made an assumption that thoughts of my wife and my mother paralleled similar issues for Zac, and I gradually formulated the following interpretation: I said that I agreed that in the dream he represented the idea of his father punishing him. I remarked that I was willing to go out on a limb and assume that he must have done something to keep his wife stirred up, instead of helping her cool off as he usually did, and that in failing to do so, he denied himself the pleasure of their sexuality that night. For the moment, my comments struck a congenial chord in Zac. We mutually constructed the idea that his success represented victory over his father, that the dream represented punishment for his success, and that he also punished himself by denying himself one of the fruits of his business victory, namely sexual relations with his wife who, in this scenario, also represented his mother.

After working on this construction for a period of time, Zac drifted into a recollection of how "physically" his mother behaved toward him during his adolescence. We had recently been discussing recollections of his mother as seductive. Now he added that he could recall "her always hugging and trying to kiss me." He then reflected at some length about his father's repeated threats to send him to reform school if he continued to "cause so much trouble." Zac commented that this could only mean his father wanted him to stop fighting with his mother because, as he noted, "I wasn't a delinquent or having that much trouble in school." I believed, at this juncture, that Zac was defensively warding off an idea that we had worked on periodically in recent weeks. Much of this recent work had centered around the construction that the savage physical fights with his mother over her supposed desire to control him actually represented a means of warding off (and gratifying at the same time) their mutual erotic desires.

At this juncture, I was filled with a familiar bittersweet feeling. Lately, as we had worked on Zac's oedipal issues, I was able to re-experience freely many of my own, and I knew I was about to do so again or that I was already doing so unconsciously. This state is a supple and generally pleasant one for me, although the issues are still painful and so the experience is a bit threatening and definitely bittersweet. When Zac recalled that his father told him at age 13 or 14 that it would be best for all if he left home, I remembered a feeling of relief and a thought that all was for the best when my parents separated and my father left home when I was 14. Here I began to remember my father's financial and emotional difficulties at that time and how later, through analysis, I learned how overwhelmed I was. I remarked to Zac that his Dad had signaled that he did not have the resources to tolerate his son's competitive strivings. This deficit reinforced Zac's guilt and anxiety so much that he experienced an over-whelmed state. From the beginning of his analysis, Zac reported puzzling, overwhelmed feelings in adolescence.

I then experienced fond memories of my analyst's insistent interpretations of the traumatic impact of my parents' divorce. I recalled him hammering at the theme that I believed I had won an oedipal victory. I remembered the academic and artistic successes of my adolescence, and I re-experienced the erotic excitement that accompanied frequent dinners with my mother. We would meet at restaurants at the end of our workdays. There we were, two tired but accomplished people. This was clearly a re-creation of my fantasied oedipal victory.

Zac concluded that due to his attraction for his mother, there could be no resolution possible with his father. I heartily chimed in, "Yes, I can just picture it, a day when all goes well for you. Dad opens the door, there is peace at home, you and Mom are not fighting, in fact she is even sitting on your lap." He roared in agreement, and I laughingly said, "Maybe the two of you are drinking martinis. You turn to Dad and say, 'Hi Pop! By the way, I earned five grand today after school.' " Zac, in a hushed tone said, "You know, a scene like that actually hap-pened."

He then told this story. When he was 17, Zac ran away from home during the summer break and found work at a local resort. His parents "tolerated" his behavior. One night he entered a bar with a woman in her thirties (his mother's age) whom he had been dating. They ordered drinks. He told me, "Amazingly, my parents walked in and saw me sitting there drinking with her. When I later went to the bathroom, my father followed me in and said, 'Now you've gone completely wild. When the summer ends you're going to the Army or to reform school, but you're going to be out of the house!' "

Zac and I shared shock and dismay over this recollection and ended the hour discussing it. I felt a bit uneasy as if all was going too well, and I remember wondering as our time came to a close whether in our next session Zac would react to my useful interpretations as a competitive victory for me. This had been a recently emerging pattern.

The subjective life of the therapist plays a powerful role in shaping transference. Perhaps Racker's (1968) idea that the analyst's countertransference determines the patient's transference carries this idea to an extreme. However, it is entirely possible that another male analyst might have fostered a mother transference instead of the father transference of this analysis. Or a withholding analyst, in the name of abstinence, might have stimulated a withholding father transference. The impact of the therapist's subjectivity affects the entire shape and form of the treatment.

When the therapist was distracted or uninterested in the beginning of the hour, he may have been resonating through counterresistance to Zac's discomfort about highly conflictual issues. We emphasize strongly that the therapist was distracted for reasons of his own and that subjective responses should not be looked at as simply reactive to what is going on in the patient, which assumes that the therapist's subjective life is, or should be, subordinate to that of the patient. Such an assumption could mean that the therapist has virtually no subjective life of his own during the therapeutic encounter.

The analyst brought into Zac's analysis his own fantasies toward his wife, his memories of his parents' divorce, his attitudes toward both parents, and his recollection of his encounters with his analyst. In recent years we have become familiar and comfortable with the idea that such fantasies are helpful in understanding our patients. But we are now proposing another step, namely that the therapist's life and times actively shape and affect the nature of the patient's transference.

A strong meta-communication occurs from the therapist to Zac that in effect says, "I too have lived through such conflicts and believe they can be tolerated and understood. I am not afraid to be, and I want to be, in the center of a reliving of them." When the therapist constructed the scene of Zac's father returning home to find his son and wife drinking martinis together, he was speaking from deep within his own similar subjective experience. Such an interpretive stance carries with it an authenticity that deepens the treatment in several ways, which we highlight throughout our discussions.

2

Intersubjectivity in Clinical Practice

WHAT IS THE BASIC RELEVANCE OF INTERSUBJECTIVITY?

The basic relevance of intersubjectivity has multiple aspects. It is the fundamental psychological explanation for the psychotherapeutic process. First, intersubjectivity maintains that psychotherapy is mutual, that is, it is an interaction, an exchange occurring between two people and about two people. Much of this interaction is unconscious. Second, it emphasizes that each individual is constructed both by himself and by the other during the process of interaction. Clearly, an individual has lived a life before meeting the therapist. However, the idea that the patient has a fixed set of self and object relations that he will live out inexorably in the therapy, as if they came off a template, no matter who the therapist is, seems oversimplified and leaves the therapist out of the equation.

People come to therapy with internal schemata of self and object that interact with their counterparts in the therapist, producing new relations (not just re-editions) that through therapy shed light on earlier ways of organizing life. The patient's old ways have multi-potentials for expression in the new setting. The desires and needs of the therapist partially determine the form they assume.

Intersubjectivity, as the primary grounding theory of psychotherapy, does not require that the stories told by other established theories of psychological development and function be abandoned. A collision with these theories occurs when they imply that there is an isolated mind that develops independently of an intersubjective process. Intersubjectivity has some very definite implications for any developmental scheme. Our clinical experience strongly suggests that all persons, from the beginning of life, develop as partners in an intersubjective matrix.

Intersubjectivity provides an opportunity for further development of the theory of psychotherapy. Traditional concepts can be retained or eliminated in accordance with their compatibility with intersubjective principles. For example, the idea of the therapist as a neutral observer who stays outside of the field and does not bring problems that require him or her to change gives way to the view that the therapist is an integral part of a complex, unique relationship. In contrast, traditional concepts about oedipal and preoedipal conflict, and deficits in self-development, are compatible with an intersubjective approach.

Study of the invariable mutuality and co-creation of the psychotherapeutic process will inevitably produce changes in how psychotherapy is conceived and practiced. The implications for change that emerge from such an understanding of psychotherapy are numerous, and we illustrate them throughout this book.

HOW IMPORTANT IS THE PSYCHOTHERAPIST'S SUBJECTIVITY IN THE THERAPEUTIC PROCESS?

Intersubjectively informed theory accords the therapist's subjectivity a level of importance that is equal to the patient's subjectivity. And this is true whether the therapist and/or the patient is aware of it. Clearly then, the therapist's subjectivity is an essential component, a sine qua non of therapy.

All human transactions are intersubjective in nature. This principle also applies to psychotherapy. It follows from this idea that the more the participants in therapy are aware of their joint subjective contribution, the richer the therapeutic experience will be.

WHAT ARE THE DISTINGUISHING CHARACTERISTICS OF INTERSUBJECTIVELY INFORMED PSYCHOTHERAPY?

All psychotherapy, however labeled, arises from an intersubjective matrix. This is true even though both therapist and patient may be unaware of it. However, therapy without an intersubjective understanding may vary widely. For instance, a therapist without such sophistication but who has a textured, subtle, intuitive appreciation of human relations will achieve a therapeutic situation that closely resembles a consciously sophisticated intersubjective therapy. In contrast, another therapist who is also unaware of intersubjectivity may, due to unconscious stumbling blocks such as unintegrated aggression, create a therapeutic situation that a thoughtful third party would perceive as drastically different from a consciously intersubjective therapy.

Intersubjective theory tends to accentuate the differences that exist among therapists and therapies. Conventional theory would stimulate a tendency toward conformity, toward an ideal of all therapies becoming alike, at least in some ways. This conforming tendency might be evident in an attempt to require that all therapies pass through the same phases. Or the conforming tendency might be evident in the requirement that the therapist strive to be the same with all his or her patients and that the technique of all therapists be identical. This is what Gill (1982) deplores as the disruptive striving for pure technique.

In conventional therapy, the conforming tendency usually revolves around a positivistic notion that specific material lies waiting in the patient's mind for the analyst and the patient to uncover. Presumably, the truth lies hidden from both parties due to the patient's resistances. The conventional approach valorizes the therapist's silence as a tool that permits the eventual expression of the hidden truths.

In contrast, the intersubjectively informed therapist views the silence as a form of interaction and assumes that the therapist is making a statement to the patient through the silence. The interactive field is opened up by viewing silence as an activity of the therapist, rather than as an external tool that the therapist somehow applies as if he were not involved in the field. With this awareness the therapist can then ask himself what his desire to be silent means and whether it is helpful at this moment. For example, the therapist's silence may be stating: "I know that you need to be with me in the safety of silence, to think your thoughts, and to develop a true sense of yourself."

The intersubjectively informed therapist enjoys a much higher degree of ambiguity than his conventional counterpart. For example, he realizes that his spoken word may be the carrier of radically different submerged messages of which he is consciously unaware. Another example would be the therapist who realizes that while his behavior appears superficially neutral, he is engaged in a powerful enactment. This greater tolerance for ambiguity enables the therapist to engage more freely in role responsiveness (Sandler, 1976), and to offer more open and tentative interpretations, since his theory does not bind him to unrealistic perfectionism. Thus, the therapy might appear more dialogical and less stilted in a monological way. Here is a case illustration of some of the points just elaborated:

(RJF) A middle-aged therapist was analyzing a slightly younger man. The patient was a brilliant businessman who would characteristically build a business to great success and then would inevitably undo the success, causing great loss for himself and those depending on him.

In the session under consideration, the patient was his usual self. He reported a dream in which he is in a foreign castle, with the therapist present as a protective escort. He believes soldiers there are shooting and killing people at random. The patient takes out a 38-caliber gun. Nevertheless, the police overpower him. He then awakens.

The analyst repeatedly attempted to obtain the patient's associations to the dream, but he was regularly foiled. Instead, he noticed that the patient seemed to want to talk only of large houses and estates. At this level the session could have been seen as highly resistant in nature.

When the analyst discussed the case with a consultant, it became apparent that an active conflict was occurring between the patient and the analyst. Had the analyst realized this conflict during the session, he might have behaved differently. The analyst wished to obtain associations to the dream, whereas the patient wanted to talk about real estate, as part of an accumulating, ambitious desire. In his wish to garner associations, the analyst was enacting his similar accumulating, ambitious wishes.

The initial impression of resistance to the analyst and the analysis would have been a conventional formulation, even though basically an intersubjective process was occurring of which neither party was aware. The later consultation indicated some of the intersubjective factors that were operating from both sides. Basically, the session was fundamentally intersubjective, and only with the later appraisal did our understanding become intersubjectively informed. When therapy becomes intersubjectively informed, it undergoes a transformation as illustrated by the following:

Several days later another consultation on the session occurred. The situation in which the patient and the analyst were pursuing different aims was reviewed. Initially in this consultation, we both assumed, as in the previous consultation, that intersubjective awareness, had it been available, might have helped the analyst achieve greater thematic congruence during the session.

However, as we strove to deepen our understanding, we came to feel that the analyst had perceived the patient's need to experience a strong father who could encourage and tolerate some necessary rebellion and competitiveness in the relationship. The patient was arguing and bantering, and the analyst in essence played the role of the straight man. There was an enactment that communicated acceptance of the patient's rebellious and competitive feelings. The patient's father, who was known as the "hanging judge," envied his son's aggressiveness and would never have tolerated such behavior.

The analyst had some similar need for a strong, accepting father so that he could quite powerfully participate in a competitive conflict in which, unconsciously, each took the role of father and son to the other's son and father. This more sophisticated intersubjective analysis presumes that the analyst's intuition serves the therapy best by engaging in the conflict. Such engagement is preferable to an intermediate and partial intersubjective understanding that there was conflict, but that the conflict needed to be terminated in order to restore a more harmonious climate to the analysis.

DOES INTERSUBJECTIVITY DESTROY
OR REFINE DEFINITIONAL
DIFFERENCES BETWEEN PATIENT
AND THERAPIST?

We have no doubts about the influence of an intersubjective perspective upon therapist and patient. It increases consciousness. This effect increases humanness and inevitably increases differentiation and individuation. In the context of therapy, this means a more clearly defined patient and a more clearly defined therapist. While their common humanity is developed and appreciated more fully, their role distinctions are also achieved more completely, and thus their differences are etched more sharply.

Although intersubjectively informed therapy de-emphasizes the formal differences between patient and therapist, it always enhances the fundamental differences between them. This is so because intersubjective processes result in increasing self-consciousness and a growing distinctiveness of the personality. Yet, the intersubjective process does entail boundary blurring associated with profound closeness of the two parties, in which their differences are obscured; however, the outcome is greater differentiation. The following case illustrates this point:

(JMN) In my work with a married actress who is the mother of two young children, we have often experienced moments or periods in which a benign fusion or merger occurs during which clear awareness of our differences is lost. For example, she had a dream in which a girl is being raped at knifepoint. As she talked about the dream, I thought of my early terror of my mother's knife, which was used for killing animals for food, and I recalled how the patient had expressed the wish to slice the balls off the man who actually raped her when she was in late adolescence. She fell silent, and I felt it appropriate to share with her some of my thoughts about her. When I reminded her of the trauma of the actual rape and of her father's earlier assaultive behavior, she became furious with me for "forcing" her to think and talk about these earlier events. In this anger, she regarded me as the rapist. So we were both confused and polarized, and each felt threatened and endangered by the other.

From this powerful set of interactions, which represented crucial re-enactments of each of our earlier life traumas, we each achieved an enhancement of our respective self-consciousness and a greater degree of differentiation.

IS THE CONCEPT OF PROJECTIVE IDENTIFICATION COMPATIBLE WITH AN INTERSUBJECTIVE PERSPECTIVE?

Projective identification originally had a strict Kleinian meaning. Over the years, it has enjoyed a growing popularity among psychoanalytically oriented psychotherapists, and the term has become more liberally defined and became largely separated from its Kleinian metapsychological roots.

Projective identification means that one person attempts to rid himself of a painful psychological state by behaving in such a way as to produce the feelings in the other person in the relationship. In consequence, the recipient begins to experience consciously the psychological state of the sender, and the sender is thereby freed of the unpleasant feelings and thoughts.

Projective identification is a clear manifestation of intersubjectivity. That is, it is an expression of how the subjectivity of one person influences the subjectivity of the other, with a change occurring in the subjective state of both parties. The name projective identification and the clinical event that it describes both have a very dramatic quality.

In typical usage, the patient "puts into" the therapist an unwelcome affect—such as anger—or an inner self-representation or object representation. The patient recognizes the affect or representation in the therapist and ascribes the source to the therapist, thereby avoiding recognizing the origin of the process in himself. The therapist initially believes that the projection first arose in him, until he comes to realize that it is really the patient's affect that he, the therapist, is experiencing.

Once the therapist realizes that he has been participating in the process of projective identification, he becomes able to extricate himself from the process and therefore to direct his attention to the patient's need to engage in projective identification.

Although we recognize that therapists often become participants in the patient's emotions and that such participation has defensive significance for the patient, we prefer not to employ the term projective identification.

We appreciate, even insist, that patient and therapist continuously influence the feelings and thoughts of one another. However, we also insist that the processes that result in such influences are surpassingly complex and are never reducible to a simple formula such as projective identification. The simplicity of the concept may lead the therapist to a premature, false sense of complete comprehension of the patient–therapist transaction. In this way, the therapist's necessary, continued search for more complete understanding may be aborted. This is a way in which the loss of ambiguity in the therapist's mind may entail a net loss for the therapy.

3

Roles of Patient and Therapist from an Intersubjective Standpoint

ARE PATIENT AND THERAPIST CO-EQUAL IN INTERSUBJECTIVELY BASED THERAPY?

Intersubjectivity certainly tends to emphasize the equality of patient and therapist. It places collaborative work in the foreground and pushes authoritarian tendencies as far as possible into the background. The notion of the therapist having the last word becomes an absurdity.

The fact that patient and therapist are equal collaborators does not mean that they are, should be, or ever could be identical. As individual humans, they are obviously different, and their roles in therapy are quite different.

The formal role distinctions have substantive importance: the patient seeks help, the therapist offers to
provide help. In our culture, the patient pays the therapist,
and the therapist earns his livelihood from therapy. In
general, the patient's life and problems are the center of
attention and the focus of the therapeutic dialogue, while
the therapist's life and problems are an important secondary focus—but are relatively silent in the manifest
dialogue. The patient brings his associations, his dreams,
and similar experiences, while the therapist attempts to
establish patterns of meaning that transform and enhance
consciousness in the patient. The patient's prime expertise
in therapy is his own background and present, as well as
his detailed knowledge of the manifest aspects of his
presenting and other problems. Using innate abilities and
driven by self-protective needs, the patient does develop
expertise in understanding the unconscious thoughts and
feelings of the therapist, but the patient's main focus is
upon himself. The therapist's psychological life is also
important, but it must share the therapist's attention with
his absorption in the patient's life and problems, his
background of study, his previous and other current
therapeutic activity, the trials and tribulations of his daily
life, and his conceptual interests as they impinge on this
therapy. The therapist thus brings professional expertise
to the encounter. Yet, this expertise has no valid relation
to authoritarian claims that therapists sometimes mistak-
enly make—believing falsely that their expertise entitles
them to arbitrary power and status. The therapist's inferences about the patient are thus viewed as educated
assumptions that need consensual validation.

Relinquishing an authoritarian stance is tightly linked to a theoretical position that abandons the positivistic notion that the analyst is an observer who remains detached from the field under observation. Theoretical systems that rest on this positivistic premise introduce an air of authoritarianism, no matter how valiantly one struggles to maintain co-equality. Inevitably, a positivistic orientation puts pressure on the therapist to provide definitive answers, and it makes him uneasy and guilty when the therapeutic situation calls for tolerance of ambiguity. In contrast, a theoretical stance that embraces the idea that the observer is a participant interacting with the field under observation makes it difficult to retain an authoritarian position. The therapist accepts a position wherein his objectivity is relative and his unavoidable subjective involvement has a theoretically supportive home. The patient unconsciously reads the therapist's unconscious intents. No matter how firmly the therapist believes his manifest formulations are true, the patient may accurately perceive a different latent meaning.

A working co-equality leading to eventual consensual agreement needs to replace what can only be described as a naive arbitrary authoritarianism. Traditional psychoanalytic theories made the analyst the ultimate knower of truth. Some contemporary psychoanalytic theories commit the same error in reverse, attributing exclusivity of truth to the patient. For example, self psychologists tend to assume that if one listens with sufficiently intense empathy, the patient's ultimate truth will be revealed. In this attitude the self psychologist remains unaware of the joint enactment. Here the therapist is being a deeply empathic and intuitive parent, and the patient gives his "truth" in childlike gratitude. Such situations are clearly two-person transactions.

Considerable asymmetry exists in a state of co-equality and mutuality. At the core, therapist and patient put forth equal emotional involvement, although the means of expressing that involvement and the returns it generates (in the form of nurturance, development, integration, and understanding) differ between the two participants.

Reviewing our work as therapists with patients, we see that virtually every interaction illustrates how, in intersubjectively informed therapy, asymmetry coexists with equality. Here is an illustrative case:

(JMN) A 55-year-old businessman, recently divorced, sought therapy to help relieve the pain of the separation from his wife, with whom he had produced and reared two grown children.

At the outset, the patient revealed that the situation was quite complex, because throughout his adult life, he had struggled with the question of whether he was gay or straight. This concern had endured unsettled despite over fifteen years of psychotherapy, which at times was intensive.

At the beginning, he was extremely anxious, although anxiety was not one of his manifest complaints. He was so anxious that his speech was quite jumbled and at times incomprehensible. Similarly, his arms and legs flailed about constantly.

Here is an example of the asymmetry of this therapy. I was impressed by the severity of his anxiety, and I resolved (silently) to attempt to understand its nature and to reduce it. I saw this as the most urgent task of the therapy. Whereas he was oblivious to his anxiety and insisted that his problem was essentially the need to make a valid decision about his sexual orientation, I, on the other hand, believed that the reduction of anxiety and the increase of a sense of self would lead to resolution of the sexual choice dilemma. I assumed that the questions about sexual identity in some obscure way expressed his more fundamental inability to be himself, and I attempted to influence the therapy in this direction. Simultaneously, I watched for signs from within myself about how my disagreement with him over the nature of his fundamental problem expressed needs of my own. I also watched for his response to my ideas and to the conflict between us.

The following also demonstrates the asymmetry of this therapy. The patient looked to me almost desperately for help and relief of his suffering. I readily accepted his demand. I told him how to free associate, I encouraged him to lie on the couch when he felt he could do so, I explained the value of dreams and how to work with them, and, very importantly, I told him that he showed only minimal experiential understanding of how his present life and his developmental years were related to one another psychologically. Fortunately, he could hear and integrate my guidance, and in one year's time we made definite therapeutic progress.

My leadership role and his role of eager follower clearly illustrate the asymmetrical nature of our early interactions. He took the role of the desperate patient while I assumed the guiding, in-charge role. With time and beneficial therapeutic development, this particular asymmetry has diminished. The patient's fear of women (including his mother) has lessened and, in obvious consequence, so have his compulsive desires for homosexual contact. He assumes more overt verbal mastery in his analysis. In fact, in a recent session, the patient vehemently disagreed with me about my formulation of the basis of his fear of his mother. He emphatically insisted that I did not understand this point, and he clearly expressed his formulation. I realized that his explanation was both parsimonious and powerful. In contrast, my interpretation seemed contrived and anemic. Clearly the early leader–follower asymmetry had by now greatly lessened. The patient was practicing his assertiveness by claiming his independence from me in my role of an idealized parental figure. Such change in the nature of the asymmetry of the therapeutic situation reflected growth in the patient. Here is another example of a joint enactment preceding, and necessary for, insight.

From the outset, I had recognized that the patient is very sophisticated in the areas of art, music, and theater. His sophistication in those areas exceeds mine. This asymmetry has often been felt by me, and, I am sure, by him. Perhaps the asymmetry along this axis represents a reversal of the parent–child roles and permits another avenue of growth. Also, he would often tell me that we have a lot of qualities in common, that he likes me — and thinks I like him, and that if we did not have a therapeutic relationship, we could be friends. This attitude indicates the co-equality in our shared experience. The co-equality that had been inherent in the therapy from the outset had now become manifest. This would have been true even if he had concluded that we had little in common and had no basis for a friendship. By co-equality, we mean equal living, or, stated differently, a co-equal investment in the relationship of our respective subjectivities.

I brought to the initial encounter with this man my characteristic father-seeking expectations. For example, when he was referred to me as a wealthy retired business-man, I probably had anticipatory fantasies of being fathered. When I met him and realized his desperation, my fantasy enabled me to become aware of precisely that need for fathering in him.

Yet, although we are intensely engaged in an inter-subjective process, our roles remain appropriately distinct; our relationship remains similarly asymmetrical. In his analysis, I know I continue to explore my relationship to my parents, as he does to his parents. Nevertheless, as his analyst, my attention, and his, focus on his concerns and preoccupations. When I am aware, from his associations, that he has tuned in to my inner world, I use this information in the service of understanding the patient and do not raise it as a subject for our mutual discussion. In other words, he occupies the central psychological space while I surround him. I also know there are nu-merous times when my sense of the relations of my parents to one another and to me drives the shared process with him. This fact does not alter my stance toward him, however, in that I remain analyst and he continues to be the patient. In different roles, each of us has different responsibilities and different opportunities. Asymmetry does not mean inequality or lack of mutuality.

Another way to view the project that he and I share is

to say that unconsciously we are absolutely co-equal—the impingement and interaction of our major life themes drive the therapy. Our co-equality otherwise reveals itself in more complex ways: our therapeutic roles are different, but have equal essential significance for the therapy.

WHAT IS SOCIAL CONSTRUCTIVISM, AND WHAT DOES IT SAY ABOUT THE RESPECTIVE ROLES OF PATIENT AND THERAPIST IN THERAPY BASED ON AN INTERSUBJECTIVE PREMISE?

Social constructivism is a hybrid term proposed by Hoffman (1991a) to denote a paradigm shift in psychoanalysis. Hoffman proposes that constructivism replace logical positivism as the fundamental paradigm in our field. In the constructivist view, no knowledge of "objective" truth exists independent of the observer (in the clinical situation) or observational system. Positivism allows the therapist to believe that he is a detached observer who does not affect the field under observation. Constructivism rests on the tenet that the observer always plays some role in shaping what he or she observes. Thus the term observation gives way to the term construction. Additionally, we therapists have previously been comfortable (via the concept of psychic reality) with the idea that the patient constructs his version of reality, first in childhood and then in therapy. Now that we see that the therapist also constructs his own version of the patient's version of reality, that the patient constructs his version of the therapist's version of the patient's version of reality, and so on, we can say that the therapist-patient pair have consciously and unconsciously co-constructed these various realities.

The term *social* emphasizes that therapy is a social interactive process, rather than an isolated solipsistic individual enterprise. This idea is in agreement with Loewald (1960) who, in his classic paper regarding the therapeutic action of psychoanalysis, stated: "By psycho-analytic process I mean the significant interactions between patient and analyst that ultimately lead to structural changes in the patient's personality" (p. 16). Once we relinquish the idea that an individual exists completely independently of the therapist (or for that matter anybody else in the world), the social aspect of life emerges forcibly and so shares equal billing in this theory's name.

Some critics fear that the constructivist therapist is kept too busy examining his own input and that he cannot allow sufficient time and space to know the patient more deeply and empathically. Yet, the more the therapist is aware of his own subjective involvement, the more comprehensive his understanding of the patient becomes.

It is sometimes argued that constructivism allows no asocial space for the very primitive or very ill patient to use the analyst nonsocially. In this view, such a patient literally comes into psychic existence through the therapist's acceptance of his or her projections and through the therapist's sustained empathy.

Hoffman (1991b), in response, invokes Racker's (1968) assertion that although the analyst has no place to stand that is fully outside his subjective involvement, there is certainly a continuum from "relative objectivity" (p. 132) to involvement in a highly subjective field in which the analyst is "caught in the grip of the field" (Stern 1991, p. 66). We would add the idea that although a patient may use the therapist upon whom to weave a sense of self, such use is not profitably viewed as asocial, that is, non-intersubjective. One person can use another as if that other possessed no needs of his own while simultaneously retaining unconscious awareness that the other person is surrendering a portion of his subjectivity (his own needs) to the task at hand.

From a technical standpoint, Hoffman (1991a) is urging that both the detached and the involved analyst not assume that their way is the right one, either in the moment or in general. He argues that the social constructivist paradigm forces the therapist, whether detached or involved, to recognize that his stance reflects the continuous co-creative process. For example, the therapist who has convinced himself that his silent empathic stance is allowing the patient full expression of his mirroring or idealizing needs, or of his "true" self, may come to learn that the patient, from his perspective, views himself as submitting to the therapist's will. The therapist then, it is hoped, will be obliged to re-examine himself to determine whether he might be camouflaging his need for dominance behind his view of himself as silently empathic. Similarly, the involved therapist, who believes he is enlivening the patient and stimulating the development of archaically arrested aspects of personality, may actually be squashing the patient's need for playful self-expression and competitiveness, or he may very well be co-conspiring with the patient to avoid reconstructing painful early life events.

The point that is driven home by the social constructivist paradigm, and one with which we agree, is that there is no safe objective stance for the therapist in which he is free of his own subjectivity. Instead, the therapist must keep confronting his own input. This does not mean, however, that he has to trip over it and that he has no time to listen quietly to the patient in a manner that would look and feel like the observing classical analyst, or the empathically attuned self psychologist, or the holding object relationist, or the quietly patient interpersonalist. Creating space for the patient to use the therapist is a co-constructive act between two individuals who are intersubjectively interwoven.

The shift from the positivistic to the constructivistic theoretical stance has implications for the major theoretical systems in psychoanalysis. Schafer's (1983, 1992) work, which also eschews a positivistic position, considers the prominent theories in our field as major "narratives." The social constructivist paradigm would also cast these theories into the role of narratives and would urge that the theoreticians' subjective input into theory building be explicated as much as possible. However, the social constructivist paradigm is somewhat silent with regard to the content of the narratives. Hoffman (1991a) notes: "The paradigm issue is independent of questions regarding the content of the primary issues in human development and the specific needs, wishes, and conflicts that are central in governing human experience and behavior" (p. 101). He acknowledges, however, that the constructivist would, by definition, be cautious about making unduly confident assertions about human nature. But he states that the constructivist position does not oppose theory building that is framed in terms of "heuristic working assumptions and hypotheses" (p. 101).

Hoffman's stance, as well as the intersubjective approach we are advancing, allows the clinician wide latitude to utilize salient aspects of the different major theoretical-narrative systems. Indeed, in accordance with Sandler's (1983) views, such a process goes on unconsciously in the analyst, and even mutually contradictory theoretical propositions drawn from differing narratives coexist and intermingle unconsciously in the therapist. There is a considerable unconscious mixture and synthesis of the major theoretical narratives in the minds of all therapists. Strong allegiance to one theoretical-narrative position may serve to camouflage powerful intersubjective forces in the therapeutic field.

In conclusion, our understanding of the interrelationships of social constructivism, intrapsychic phenomena, and the role of personal history is incomplete, and at present we must recognize and accept certain contradictions. The apparent contradictions may be a matter of level or aspect under consideration. Construction or discovery may be going on simultaneously or sequentially, but the operation of two separate yet interpenetrating processes may not be sufficiently evident to the participants.

DOES THE THERAPIST'S SUBJECTIVE
LIFE ALWAYS PLAY A ROLE IN THE
GENERATION OF THE PATIENT'S
FEELINGS, ATTITUDES, AND
THOUGHTS?

Answer. The basic answer is *yes.* Sometimes this ever-present influence is very apparent. At other times it may seem very faint, almost undiscernible. Examples of these two extremes should be helpful. They illustrate how the therapist's subjectivity generates responses of the patient and leads to discovery of traumatic memories.

Example 1:

(RJF) As Gail spoke about her fears of a business meeting with Donna, I remembered childhood scenes of listening to my mother endlessly complaining about her lot in life to my grandmother. Often unable to extricate myself from witnessing these frustrating interchanges, I would come to feel both shut out and hopeless that my mother would ever resolve her worries and be happy. I now found myself feeling similarly with Gail. After analyzing the matter for a while, I told her that while we certainly could continue to talk about competitive feelings toward Donna and their relation to similar ones toward her mother and sister, I now believed such constructions would get us nowhere.

Gail was at first surprised by my remark because she quickly noted how important the subject had been of late and how freeing our discussions of it over recent months had been to her. She lamented haltingly that she wished she could write down some of my interpretations about competitiveness with her mother and sister to offset the confusion about these issues she often felt after sessions. I felt like a priest being asked to dispense a catechism. Gail announced that she felt like a little girl with a daddy who knew everything and who would take care of her. However, when she contemplated what our therapeutic relationship would be like if she were also to know what I knew, she became uncomfortable. Simultaneously I pictured myself teaching one of my psychoanalytic seminars.

The last class in this course had been a challenging, competitive one, and I allowed myself to assume that Gail too would experience strong competitiveness with me were she to allow herself to learn what I had to teach in the analysis. I then constructed this idea in an interpretive form and presented it to Gail.

As she free associated to my interpretive remarks, Gail began to express her conviction that I would never tolerate her equality with me and the challenges that she could mount. She was convinced that "you will simply wash your hands of me and walk away." Thus the only solution she could conceive was to have me dominate her. We had discussed this type of pattern between her and her mother many times before, but this new slant on it, filtered through our relationship, led to a new memory. She recalled that at an early age her mother would summon her at night and "force" Gail to remove her (mother's) makeup, brush her hair, and fetch her night-gown. There were erotic undertones to Gail's feelings as she related the nightly ritual. Although Gail believed this form of servitude was short-lived, its "discovery" opened up for analysis over the next segment of time similar traumatic moments that eventually led to a deeper recon-struction of both her hatred for and her homosexual longings toward her mother.

The above example demonstrates a case in which the therapist's subjectivity played an active initiating role. A dialogue that began about the patient's subtle attitudes toward an intimate other turned into an interesting and important puzzle that led, through the mutual influence of patient and therapist upon each other, to constructions of the transference relationship, which eventually were followed by the "discovery" of long-forgotten events.

Example 2:

(JMN) A number of years ago I treated an unmarried writer in her late thirties. She had just gone through her latest severe regression. In these states, she became suicidally depressed, lost all sense of a coherent self, and split into multiple personalities. She would cling to me in despair and anger over her frustrated needs to be close.

Typically when she made significant gains, she then regressed. In this incident, several factors converged to induce the loss of integrative capability. One key element was that she assumed (with only the merest shred of reality as far as I could see) that I had slighted her by not responding more enthusiastically to some of her recent remarks to me.

After two chaotic days, she began reconstitution and was now behaving "reasonably." As she resumed her detailed but halting explanation of what had happened, I began to feel annoyed by the somewhat didactic and blaming hints in her remarks. This alerted me to remind her of something that I had recently been pointing out, namely, that she had fixed ideas about me that I thought were incorrect and that these were part of her defense system against becoming conscious of the trauma by her mother (and father). Her insistent reiteration of how I failed her because I could not literally be her mother epitomized her disorder of thought.

Her recent extremely disturbed behavior constituted her subjective contribution. My basic urge to help her derived from a longstanding desire to help my family members out of their pain. When I felt she was thwarting this wish by adopting a false explanatory stance, I became angry. I then could recognize the aggression in her behavior and realize that she was re-enacting another of her multiple traumas, and, in turn, this realization helped me appreciate the defensive nature of her distorted thinking and explaining.

This rather complex interpretive process illustrates how a meaning is created in a session, relying heavily on the therapist's subjective experience.

After this complex intersubjective crisis receded and the patient had the benefit of the above insight that she and I had jointly created, she experienced a "discovery." At the height of her disturbance, the patient had sunk limply from the couch to the floor, and, among other acts, she pounded her forehead with her fists and also struck her forehead against the floor repeatedly.

When she came to her session the next day, one of her first actions was to show me very insistently that she now had large black and blue bumps on her forehead. I asked her why she needed to display these to me, and she replied that her behavior expressed the hope that her mother would make it better.

Then, I asked why she had pounded her head so hard. At this point, she recovered the memory that this was the exact location of her father's hammer attack on her head.

This new insight was the patient's discovery or, one could say, approximate re-creation — or approximate creation — of a memory that very closely resembled the original event. However, it arose in crucial relation to the previous highly reconstructive interpretation of defense against traumatic memories, and this earlier interpretation was developed in a very constructivist manner.

Perhaps construction and discovery represent ideal poles of what is really a continuum and that in reality we only deal with mixtures of each. Thus we could say that discovery results from construction and that from the discovery comes new construction. Discovery, which so often means (using the old positivistic archaeological model) retrieval of a piece of the past, demonstrates the existence and the importance of history in the patient's mind. And discovery demonstrates that history has a central place in psychotherapy.

Both of these clinical examples illustrate the everpresent influence of the therapist's subjectivity and the importance of co-construction between patient and therapist. At the other extreme, a patient may have a terrible nightmare and come to his session the next day bursting with eagerness to discuss the dream and its possible meanings. Here one might understandably question whether the therapist had any generating role in the patient's feelings, attitudes, and thoughts at this time. Nevertheless, the answer should still be affirmative, for the following two obvious reasons, at least: (1) the nightmare itself is in part an expression of the whole therapeutic experience thus far, including the therapist's subjective contributions, and (2) the patient enters the therapeutic scene and immediately responds to the therapist's impinging expectation of the patient's communications. Therefore, all the human psychological forces emanating from the therapist will play some generating role in whatever the patient does in the session, however inapparent this influence may be.

DOES THE PATIENT'S SUBJECTIVE LIFE
ALWAYS PLAY A ROLE IN THE
THERAPIST'S FEELINGS, ATTITUDES,
AND THOUGHTS?

The phenomenon of countertransference must be invoked to answer this question. *Countertransference* is the term that Freud introduced to account for the patient's influence upon the therapist's psychological state. So, an obvious "yes" to the question might seem sufficient. Actually, however, the patient has a continuous influence upon the therapist and not only in terms of specific and intermittent thoughts, attitudes, and feelings of the therapist. At all times, all aspects of the therapist's ongoing psychological experience are to some extent, large or small, being influenced and shaped by the patient's impinging psychological life.

The reciprocal influence of the subjectivity of the patient and therapist upon one another is continuous. This means that often such influence is not readily discernible, even when it is a powerfully significant factor in the therapeutic process.

In the previous case of the writer who was prone to severe regressions, the tempestuous transactions readily lend themselves to analysis that reveals how the patient's subjectivity influences the analyst.

The patient desperately sought a good mother, but she usually tended to find the bad mother. I was regularly attempting to make the miserable mother happy, but in doing so, I was vulnerable to the complaint or dissatisfaction of the unhappy other. The patient met my approach with direct or indirect indications of her feelings that I was insensitive, indifferent, or rejecting. (She selected these behaviors from among a broad spectrum of positive and negative responses on my part — thus creating what is referred to as the negative transference.) This touched my vulnerable spot, and I became defensive. She perceived my hurt feelings and then had the evidence to support her dismal conviction. This sequence of events might then grow into a major decompensation. Or if I could analyze my subjective experience rapidly enough, I would be able to resume an empathic attitude, respond to her pain, and restore relative tranquility.

Some therapists would call this an example of projective identification. We prefer, for reasons already cited, not to employ the term.

It seems clear in such an example as this that the process of reciprocal influence is a seamless one and that the patient is influencing the therapist continuously, as is the therapist continuously influencing the patient.

WHAT BASIC PRINCIPLES SHOULD
GUIDE THE THERAPIST'S RESPONSE
TO THE PATIENT'S ANGER,
LOVE, SUSPICIONS, DREAD, OR
OTHER EMOTIONS DIRECTED TO
THE THERAPIST?

The answer is emphatically that the therapist should consistently assume that he has *some* contribution to whatever emotion the patient feels toward him. This invariable assumption eventually feels to the therapist like a natural, ever-present part of the therapist's subjective and evaluative participation in the therapeutic process.

In this stance, the therapist spontaneously and comfortably reflects upon his subjective state and readily follows the associative pathways that become available. It is therapeutically profitable to explore these inner pathways before making any conventional interpretation of the meanings of the patient's emotions in the therapeutic transaction. Such a policy drastically diminishes the possibility that an interpretation to the patient will have self-aggrandizing or self-exculpating meaning and purpose for the therapist. If the same interpretations still seem valid to the therapist after optimal self-reflections, it can then be offered to the patient with some measure of confidence that its defensive meaning for the therapist has been greatly diminished and that it is now an honest and valid interpretation (construction) of meaning within the intersubjective field.

The following example is especially interesting because it is an ambiguous communication by the patient that induces an ambiguous response in the therapist. In turn this response leads to some valuable insight.

(JMN) The patient is a 42-year-old single female who is quite sophisticated regarding matters psychotherapeutic. Often she makes remarks such as "You are the most brilliant psychoanalyst in the world." She makes such statements with a teasing smile. Although it is obvious that these remarks express tender, affectionate feelings, they also seem to contain other elements that are difficult to grasp or define. I hear these comments with mixed feelings. They amuse me; I feel flattered, but also feel uncomfortable and puzzled. Even though I realize that these remarks are at least half-jokes by the patient, I still find myself secretly welcoming them. This recognition reminds me of my lifelong need for praise from my family and the issues that underlie and coexist with this need. Among others I include here my search for my father's love and my guilty need for reassurance from my mother and sisters because of my sexual and hostile feelings to them.

My strong impression is that the patient is not only stimulating such feelings in me but that I am also conveying the need for such remarks to her, and thus contributing to the characteristic remarks that she makes. Usually when she makes such a comment, I simply cast her an amused and quizzical smile that lets her know that I do not accept the remark at face value and that I regard it as very ambivalent. I refrain from quick interpretation because I regard it as very important that I explore my inner response to her remark quickly and thoroughly. Even if I made some simple interpretation such as "The remark seems ambivalent," I think the interpretation would deflect my associative focus from me to her, and I would abort my discomfiture. This would reduce my ultimate understanding of the meaning of her remark to me and to her.

In fact, her remark does not lend itself to direct interpretation. Instead it makes me aware of nuances in her attitude and behavior that help me orient my basic attitude and comments toward her. I am able with the knowledge gained from reflecting on her characteristic remarks to provide more textured response to the patient's verbal and nonverbal behavior, especially in relation to her ambivalent attitudes toward members of her developmental family.

To make a specific interpretation of this characteristic, very ambivalent comment would be to negate the essential quality of her experience and her communication. It would also negate my contributions to her experience and communication.

4

Intersubjectivity and the Therapist's Self-disclosure

WHAT IS SELF-DISCLOSURE?

Disclosure is defined as laying bare, revealing. *Self-disclosure* then means self-revelation. As therapists, we are aware that different reasons and motives for self-disclosure may exist, and we also know that in life, we often reveal ourselves without being conscious or aware that we are doing so.

Therefore, we can confidently assert that in therapy, therapists are at all times revealing some aspect of themselves, so they are self-disclosing even when they provide no explicit information about themselves. This is an unconscious, continuous, implicit, and inevitable process.

IS INTERSUBJECTIVITY SYNONYMOUS
WITH A TALKATIVE, FREELY AND
DELIBERATELY SELF-REVEALING
THERAPIST?

The answer is an emphatic *no*. Intersubjectivity is a fundamental principle of human relations and meaning. The attempt to correlate it with volubility or garrulousness constitutes a crude trivialization of the concept. The following two examples illustrate powerful, nonverbal, silent intersubjective moments: (1) a man silently hands a rose lovingly to a woman and (2) a mother refuses to talk to her 4-year-old boy for an entire day because the child was "bad." Intersubjectivity promotes therapist flexibility, and, in many instances, this flexibility may result in a quieter, less intrusive therapist.

The silent therapist is not necessarily aloof or detached. The silence may actually enhance the underlying intersubjective intensity occurring between patient and therapist, yet with minimal violation of the patient's own thoughts and feelings. The following illustration is from an analytic supervision.

(JMN) A 30-year-old male patient lay on the couch, talking freely, and, as always, feeling very distant from his laconic male analyst who rarely spoke. When he did speak, the analyst would make an interpretation that seemed obscure in meaning and critical in tone. The patient was always uncomfortable in the presence of his analyst, having the impression that the analyst disliked and/or disapproved of him. This state of affairs persisted unchanged throughout several months of treatment, until the therapist began to understand his own fears of intimacy.

This is an example of therapy in which the silent, enigmatic therapist is withholding warmth. He is sending powerful messages to the patient that say, "I am withholding warm, loving feelings because I fear the intimacy of it all. I believe that if I spoke more to you, I would become known to you, and you would become known to me. This kind of intimacy frightens me, so I avoid it."

A situation like this one illustrates how a silent therapist can be a distant, withholding therapist. But silence does not always have this meaning, as in this following example:

(JMN) A 30-year-old single, female, junior television executive came to see me for analysis. She reported that she had only recently come to Los Angeles, that she was lonely, and that she was depressed. She was very preoccupied with her family, who lived elsewhere. Her parents had their home in the Midwest, where her father was a writer and her mother was a business executive. She had a brother several years older who lived in a southern city. The brother suffered with chronic drug dependency, work instability, and disabling conflicts in intimate relationships.

Early in the analysis, the patient complained a great deal about her parents. Her basic complaint was that when she was 15, they had separated. Although the parents reunited after an extended separation, the experience was deeply disturbing and scarring to the patient. She felt also that something was wrong in her relationship to her father. Nothing traumatic had ever happened between them, but she harbored a chronic sense of discomfort around him and she felt that at least some of this feeling originated in her father's attitudes. Furthermore, during late adolescence, when the patient had a neurotic desire to have plastic surgery to reduce her breast size, her mother supported her in this wish, and the patient had the surgery. Later, the patient came to regret this action, and she now blamed her mother for not trying to prevent the surgery.

Of course, there was much more to her story, even in the earliest few hours. It poured out freely. My verbal activity was limited to occasional facilitating comments. My initial, and subsequent, impression was that she was a subtle, sensitive person with a basic desire to know her own psychological truths. A quality of warmth and trusting candor quickly permeated the atmosphere.

In one of our early sessions, she told me that she had experienced difficulty finding a therapist with whom she could feel comfortable. It was not surprising to me that she had left one previous therapist because, as she complained about her mother, he called the mother a "bitch." She assumed that he thought, in his active siding with her about her mother, that he was being supportive and empathic. Nothing of the kind. Instead, he was undermining her, depriving her of the condition of safety in which she could express and explore her hostility to her mother without sacrificing her love for her.

My relative silence, while at the same time conveying nonverbal acceptance and encouragement, enabled her to release and later resolve her ambivalence to her mother in a hitherto unprecedented way.

In this case, my silence was an intersubjectively informed way of being with her, and it helped her become engaged in a powerful therapeutic experience. In my silence I was saying to her subtextually that I was not trying to take her love from her mother for myself. This was unlike the previous therapist who, with his pseudo-empathic remarks, was perhaps trying to divert her love for her mother to himself.

In the following example implicit self-disclosure occurred beyond the analyst's control, and explicit self-disclosure became necessary in order to save the analysis.

(RJF) A beginning psychoanalytic candidate was skillfully analyzing a bright, very troubled 40-year-old unmarried man at a very low fee. When the case was first presented to me as the supervisor, the patient struck us both as a man without an identity. His sense of a stable self with any degree of strength was poorly developed, and he mainly defined himself through his attachment to whichever woman was currently taking care of him. The patient bemoaned the fact that he was working as an assistant restaurant manager, and he was quite depressed about his lack of any career plan.

A strong idealizing mother transference dominated the opening six months of analysis. The patient on many occasions stated, "This is my only chance, it's my last chance," and looked to the analyst as a strong helper. The main interpretive work centered on the patient's fears of closeness that he equated with domination and control similar to the iron grip on the family held by his mother.

The slow and steady work of analysis was interrupted by a series of life events that we believed were largely beyond the patient's control. First, his girlfriend insisted on moving to a suburb forty-five minutes from the analyst's office, after she got a job in that area. The patient grudgingly followed her, although he seethed with rebellion. Then, his car broke down, but he still managed to scramble and attend his analytic sessions. A new and promising job as a restaurant manager temporarily buoyed him, but this position soon turned into a dead end for him. The owner delayed his salary payments for long periods of time, and he had no control of his hours, which were dictated to him capriciously. The patient passively endured long hours with only a promise of pay. He began to miss occasional analytic hours. Our hypothesis was that he was disorganizing, and this in turn caused the absences. We believed that the absences were also pleas for help from the analyst and an expression of his rebellion toward the analyst's maternal authority.

The analyst, afraid of his own and of the patient's aggression, waited to tell the patient about a one-week vacation until less than two weeks remained before the departure. The patient was crushed, and, in a quasi-delusional manner, insisted the analyst was betraying him and should not leave him. Shortly before the vacation, his girlfriend broke up with him (an event that he provoked), and he was temporarily homeless. His plea for help extended to the work sphere, where he complained of feeling disorganized and desirous of quitting his noxious job, but felt too helpless to do so without the analyst's presence. We decided that the treating analyst would call the patient several times during his vacation. In retrospect, we are convinced that these calls, which were of brief duration, helped the patient tolerate the absence and remain in the city. Otherwise, he would have fled to a resort town several thousand miles away where he had spent long years doing menial labor, hanging out and drinking and using drugs with his friends.

After the vacation, the patient continued to insist that the analyst never should have left. He expressed a strong feeling of betrayal and had no insight into the more rational side of life, namely, that analysts take vacations. The analyst was rattled by and angry at the patient's attitude and was only partially able to understand his own anger in terms of his own subjectivity. In his childhood, the analyst had often appeased his domineering and controlling mother. Fortunately, he now had his own analysis in which to work on these issues that were being activated in him by the patient's behavior and attitude.

The final and crucial phase of our story pits the disillusioned and frightened patient against the partially angry and confused analyst. The patient now stated that fully resuming the analysis in person rather than by telephone meant exposing himself to the certainty of being controlled and betrayed. He began to miss sessions, allegedly rationalizing his actions as largely due to his chaotic life circumstances (which, in fact, were now stabilizing). He was intermittently able to acknowledge his fears and was especially able at times to discuss the sense of control he believed he gained by deliberately missing sessions.

The analyst was able to help the patient slowly settle down, and gradually order began to return to his life. The anger at the analyst's betrayal was interpreted, but the

analyst now participated with less enthusiasm and conviction than before. Instead, he continued to bristle and rebel
at being seen by the patient as the one who had hurt him
and "done something wrong." At this juncture, the patient
was attending half of his sessions in person, and most of
the others were conducted by phone. He was slowly
coming back into the office.

Finally the analyst could contain his anger no longer,
and one day when the patient was in the office for a
session the analyst unconsciously ended the hour ten
minutes early. The patient called afterward to express his
hurt and incredulity. I, as the supervisor, firmly agreed
that the analyst's action had to be acknowledged. I agreed
with the analyst's decision to tell the patient that his reason
for ending the hour early was that he was upset by the
patient's recent behavior. The analyst told this to the
patient, adding that he did not yet fully understand his
own feelings and that he would continue to make every
effort to do so.

The patient reacted in two ways. First, he felt betrayed because he believed the analyst was insisting on
"being a three-dimensional person." The patient then went
on to define such a person as one who could hurt him. He
in turn insisted that he needed a firm figure who would not
be hurt by his actions, and he defined this type of figure as
"two-dimensional." Second, we soon learned that behind
the patient's wish to elevate and idealize the analyst was a
wish to hurt him. The patient consequently felt repugnance toward himself as he realized that he held such a
desire.

Gradually, as the patient's tolerance for his own

aggression developed, he resumed regular visits. The pre-vacation pattern of submission to, and idealization of, a powerful maternal authority figure continued, but the patient became aware of his hatred of and rebellion against the analyst's authority. He began to feel it and to take responsibility for it. The feeling of repugnance over his own aggression continued.

The analyst's self-disclosure of his frustration in this case served a crucial role in the preservation of the analysis. Instead of blaming the patient, making up excuses, or avoiding the topic outright, the explicit self-disclosure allowed the analyst-patient pair to remain in authentic relation to one another.

WHAT IS META-COMMUNICATION?

In psychoanalytic psychotherapy, the term *meta-communication* designates the ideas, meanings, attitudes, and feelings that are conveyed between the two parties beyond the explicit or readily inferable exchanges. Sometimes, the meta-communications contradict and supersede the more obvious communications. A simple example would be saying "yes" while unconsciously shaking your head from side to side. At other times, meta-communications constitute a complementary or supplemental component of the total communicative action.

We assume that all the thoughts and feelings of each party in therapy are *somehow* conveyed to the other party. This assumption, if correct, means that at all times, the entire psychological world of each party—including each party's past—is accessible, in some essential way, to the other party. This may be seen as broad-band meta-communication that derives from our view that each person is immersed in the entire human universe.

Yet, meta-communication can mean a narrower band of specific communications that possess great power and significance. These meta-communications very often transcend the importance of the stated or deliberately implied communications of therapy. This does not mean that such meta-communication invariably or usually contradicts the overt communication, but its message may be more powerful and primary than that of the obvious communication. What we are describing constitutes the commonplace of therapy, that is, it occurs over and over, shaping the course of the therapy.

In the case of the 30-year-old female television executive who had terminated an earlier therapy because the male therapist had called her mother a "bitch," a recent meta-communication illustrates how such messages are inferred by the therapist and, very importantly, how they can thereby be changed into overt communication.

The patient began an analytic session with the report of a dream in which she is friendly with a girl from high school whom she disliked. She was puzzled by the dream initially. Her associations were to work difficulties, her relationship to her parents, and the growing likelihood of her marriage in the relatively near future. The unifying characteristic of her associations was her steadily increasing assertiveness in all these areas of her life.

As she spoke, my thoughts tended to go back to her

developmental history and to the early period of her analysis. That meant that I thought about how she talked of herself in very disparaging ways, calling herself a mouse, a worm, a rabbit; that is, a weak, frightened, unassertive, hiding creature. This flood of associations in me was partly stimulated by her associations to her present assertiveness. So I told her that I thought the girl she didn't like in the dream was the girl she used to be, the girl with a deficient sense of self. This was my explicit communication to her.

However, the meta-communication was my focus on how greatly she has changed as a result of her analysis. This focus was not stated when I made my original remarks to the effect that the previously disliked person in the dream was the girl she used to be.

The contrast between how the patient is currently and how she used to be continued to pervade my thinking during the next several analytic sessions while her associative themes continued as before. The focus of my thoughts remained so consistent, however, that I decided it merited explication, and I stated that for several sessions, I had been thinking how greatly she had changed. By making this statement, I had transformed the metacommunication into an explicit communication.

She felt that these thoughts accurately reflected her present situation. She then spoke of her major increase in confidence in her love relationship. The sexually exciting aspects of the previous uncertainty of the relationship have diminished as she and her lover have gained security with one another. The relationship feels much deeper. I said that probably the superficially diminished excitement paralleled the reduction of inhibition—the need for excitement having been a secondary alternative to satisfactions based upon more solid experience. This interpretation could have remained in meta-communicative form had I chosen not to make the comment. It really was optional. I chose to make the interpretation explicit because I regarded it as a corollary to my comment about the change in her due to the analysis. The additional thought that I did not mention was that the corollary observation exemplified one of an endless number of manifestations of reduced inhibitions, which then add up to a major change in her assertiveness and her sense of self. So this unstated thought remained a meta-communication. I am sure that she got the message. It simply seemed uneconomical to me to make the additional comment.

The next case is an example of explicit self-disclosure with a profound meta-communicative dimension. (RJF) Rebecca, a 49-year-old artist, was in the final stages of a career change facilitated by the success of a long analysis. Rebecca had definitely been physically abused and possibly also sexually molested by her father. The younger sister reported a definite history of sexual abuse. For Rebecca, however, the greatest trauma stemmed from her relationship with her mother, the mere thought of whom evoked a strong aversive and hateful reaction in her.

As of this writing, she and I have successfully reconstructed two levels of trauma with her mother. The first began at birth and continued until a sister was born when Rebecca was 4 years old. In this view, her mother was depressed and depleted, states of mind that were often masked superficially by her mother's complaints of a bad back. The grandparents intermittently provided collateral mothering. Nevertheless, the disturbed early relationship with the mother reflected itself in proneness to panic states and somatized anxiety—particularly in spasms in the muscles surrounding the mouth, head, and neck. The mother problem also expressed itself in a deep pervasive sense of guilt and a desire to rescue Mother. Rebecca had a screen memory that at age 4, Mother told her that she was grown up enough and that Rebecca did not need her any longer because the younger sister needed all the mothering. After age 4, a second level of trauma in their relationship ensued that persisted into adulthood and Mother's death. This trauma was the feuding contentiousness of their relationship. Rebecca was competitive and scornful of Mother and experienced Mother as envious and competitive, giving rise to Mother's penchant for always finding something to criticize in Rebecca's behavior or attire. This relationship was so noxious that by the time Rebecca was in the first grade, she attached herself to peers and "lived in their homes."

In the most recent phase of her analysis, Rebecca increasingly came to see and feel that she was missing a connection to a warm and loving "good mother." We had repeatedly traced her awesome identification with her father who, despite being deeply disturbed, was not clinically depressed and who was a functioning and moderately successful person. Where Mother was experienced as "dead," he at least represented life. And so, despite his rageful abuse, a strong but fragile bond developed between them in childhood, based almost entirely on Rebecca's identification with Father's ambitious and puritanical work habits.

I gradually came to recognize a pattern in the analysis that may have developed recently, but that may have been there all along. Perhaps I was not ready to hear it, for when I finally did, I became disturbed and felt inadequate. In short, Rebecca accused me of insensitivity to her. She believed that I lacked empathy and that I was not providing some essential form of a curative experience, captured by the idea that I did not care for her like a mother tiger aggressively protecting her cubs. As I heard each complaint in this context, I always agreed that in some essential way she was right. Even though we both came to recognize that she was searching for the perfect mother and accosting her imperfect one through her anger at me, we did agree on the significant kernel of truth in her observations of me. After each encounter, I learned more about myself. My ability to empathize with other individuals deepened incrementally. More importantly, my relationship with Rebecca deepened and became more relaxed after each of these encounters.

After each exchange with Rebecca, I felt foolish and was led to reconstruct some aspect of my angry relationship with my mother and to learn more of my resultant withholding behavior. It was based on my expectation of being used if I was forthcoming. Each time I then vowed that this would be my last act of withholding, and that henceforth I would be more open, empathic, and giving. No longer would she have to suffer my inhibited, withheld love. In turn I hoped my openness would foster some maternal base that would allow her to free herself from the crippling identification with her father.

Inevitably, despite my resolve, I could never find a way to Rebecca's heart directly (although she sensed and approved of my effort through recognition of how much I had changed—which was true in general but particularly with her). By the time the following incident occurred, all I knew for sure was that my best bet was to be as honest and authentic as possible with her. That might sound strange, like apple pie and motherhood, but I am speaking of a type of authenticity between analyst and patient that I find characterizes my work with abused and highly traumatized individuals in particular. This type of speaking from the heart lays the therapist affectively bare and blinds him cognitively—not typically a comfortable position for a therapist.

On a day between analytic sessions, Rebecca called and left a message of concern on my answering machine. She remarked that she thought my home might be endangered by a large fire that burned near the area of Los Angeles in which we both lived. I called Rebecca back and left a message on her answering machine that I was touched by her concern. I continued with the following self-disclosure: I said that while our house had been in no immediate danger, the turn the fire had threatened to take before it was contained had scared me.

Rebecca began the next session with an immediate reference to my self-disclosure. The fact that I was scared felt "confirming" to her. She then presented a string of associations to three or four people whom she talked to during the height of the fire. All of them, even the one whose house was in danger similar to mine, minimized or ridiculed her concern.

As I was thinking to myself that the depiction of these individuals sounded quite similar to her view of her parents as constantly devaluing her opinions, she rapidly shifted the topic to her intense anxiety over a recent work project setback. An individual in charge of an important department at her workplace had made a series of suggestions concerning the project on which Rebecca was working. She intellectually understood that these were meant to be helpful suggestions. She nevertheless was gripped with panic and stated that she was frozen to the point where she could not write a cogent reply to this man, whom Rebecca identified as a father figure. This anxiety persisted despite her supervisor's statement to her that she was not at all obligated to please this man and that she should proceed with her program as it had been outlined by him and others on the board of directors. In short, he said to her that this individual's comments were of no importance and that she could ignore them if she wished. In her mind, I was linked with her supervisor as somebody who supported her ability to stand up against this fantasied attack.

Rebecca's associations then took another turn as she recounted a series of recent encounters with people in which she felt mildly rejected. She then recounted the past few weeks in terms of lack of social contact, culminating in the idea that she was isolated socially and that nobody in the world cared about her.

I tentatively offered the interpretation that she seemed to be reproducing the childhood situation (that we had talked about many times) in which she felt as though her father was attacking her, but that she had to cling to him because her mother had abandoned her. Rebecca responded by stating, "That's just not enough!" She went on to remark that "this is like a phobia and I'm not unlearning it." She likened the situation to one in which she felt too scared or hopeless to enter into a trusting relationship with me or with her supervisor. In particular, she felt she could not trust us to be different than her mother, and thus, she felt doomed to stay with her dad and to submit to his attacks.

Rebecca then recalled my disclosure of fear. With great difficulty and "with a lump in my throat," she told me that she was very frightened of believing that "you love me." She added that she was equally afraid to believe I was different than her mother. We talked at some length about her fear of my love and her shame over loving, tender feelings.

Our discussion of shame over loving and tender feelings led Rebecca, at the end of the hour, to recall her parents' attitudes toward such tenderness. She said, "They would rather die in a ditch" than give in to such emotions. As she became aware of her identification with this position, we went on to analyze much of the parents' and Rebecca's combative behavior as an effort to ward off warm feelings. As the hour closed, Rebecca reiterated how important my acknowledgment of fear was to her. The explicit self-disclosure of my fear carried a multitude of metacommunications.

> ARE THE EFFECTS OF DELIBERATE
> CONSCIOUS SELF-DISCLOSURE
> ESSENTIALLY THE SAME AS, OR
> ESSENTIALLY DIFFERENT FROM, THE
> INEVITABLE SELF-DISCLOSURE THAT
> ALWAYS OCCURS DURING THERAPY?

Deliberate self-disclosure is a different phenomenon than the self-disclosure that is implicit and inherent in any human relationship. The former may be manipulative or violative if it arises from defensive motives. Yet, as the preceding case examples demonstrated, judicious self-disclosure may be crucial for the success of therapy. The mutual recognition that ensues can have a powerful facilitating effect upon the therapy.

Implicit self-disclosure, in contrast, may be seen as synonymous with the experience of getting to know someone. That is, through the thousands of communicative signals that are exchanged, each of the two parties achieves a thorough familiarity with the other. This is the reality of a relationship, and in this context, a huge array of beliefs, memories, values, ideas, and expectations in each person become knowable to the other, and innumerable influences upon each other thereby occur. This is clinical intersubjectivity in the therapeutic process—the implicit therapeutic dialogue. We are fascinated that a powerful, coherent therapeutic process goes on in an implicit way. The authenticity of each individual is at work, not distorted or distracted by the defensive conscious superstructure.

If the preceding is true, then what of the conscious, more or less explicit dialogue of therapy? Is it only a defensive, irrelevant redundancy? Not at all. At its best, verbal explication is one of the highest forms of human communication. Of course, at its worst, the overt or manifest dialogue misleads, obscures, distracts, and thus impairs the effectiveness and power of the therapeutic process. For example, the therapist who makes a dynamic formulation and who, through his verbal interventions, attempts to squeeze the patient onto his procrustean couch, is remarkably insensitive. Yet, many of us, under therapeutic stress, have committed this sin.

So what is the significance of the manifest therapeutic transactions? At their best, they are a fully resonant part of the total intersubjective field and provide a unique richness to it. Another important effect is to reduce surface anxiety sufficiently to clarify and amplify the basic meta-communication process. This anxiety reduction occurs in both parties. Metaphorically, we may see the manifest dialogue as clearing away the underbrush that obscures and reduces access to the fundamental intersubjective therapeutic transactions, that is, the deeply implicit or meta-communicative ones.

The preceding discussion clarifies the important distinctions between overt and implicit dialogue. Conscious self-disclosure is attended by an intersubjective risk of distortion or deflection of the therapeutic process. Nevertheless, at times, it may profoundly resonate with the therapeutic process.

No inference should be drawn from this discussion to the effect that the manifest dialogical contributions by the therapist are weighted toward destructiveness and that we should attempt to reduce or eliminate the overt dialogue, which includes some conscious, deliberate therapist self-disclosure. Our discussion is intended to consider the problematic aspects of the therapist's role in therapeutic conversation, without any effort to devalue such conversation.

Examples may further help demonstrate how deliberate, explicit self-disclosure differs from inevitable, implicit self-disclosure.

(JMN) First, a simple example of the latter. Patient and therapist are working vis-à-vis each other. The patient tells sadly how, as a child, one of his siblings died. He scans the therapist's face, and there he sees pain and sadness in the therapist's eyes. The patient feels moved that the therapist cares enough to react with sad feelings. But even here there is an additional important meaning that does not immediately meet the eye. Later in the session, the patient began to talk for the first time about death wishes he had harbored toward the sibling who died. These revelations indicated that the patient had perceived correctly the basic attitude of the therapist as conveyed by the lachrymose eyes. Namely, the therapist was responding to the patient's total experience of anguish, not simply to the conventionally acceptable feelings of grief. The patient therefore felt safe to share the less conventionally acceptable death wishes. It has been stated that therapists should not express sympathy when a loved one of the patient has died on the basis that such condolence might increase inhibitory guilt toward the therapist/ superego figure. Such an analysis is incorrect because it rests on a basic misconstrual of the meaning of the therapist's visible sympathy. This misconstrual is based on the assumption that the therapist feels for the patient's grief only. The correct view of the therapist's pain is that it expresses the therapist's feeling for the entire patient, not just his conventionally acceptable feelings. In fact, when the patient realized how intensely the therapist accepted *him*, he then felt free to reveal his guilt-laden death wishes toward the unfortunate sibling.

This example of implicit self-disclosure through tearful eyes tells us that similar events occur many times in every session. What is our facial expression, tone of voice, or posture when we greet the patient? Are we more or less voluble in the session? What body language do we speak in the session? Do we ask questions, listen attentively, make interpretations? Whatever our interventions, are they attuned or out of tune? The patient makes observations constantly about us and draws powerful inferences from these observations. These kinds of developments are inexorable in therapy. The therapist can neither run away nor hide from them. As the reader can appreciate, such complexities constitute a large measure of the therapeutic experience and justify what Hoffman (1991a) calls the *social constructivist* viewpoint.

Explicit, deliberate self-disclosure has more finite limits, because once we start to explore extensions of meaning of the explicit, we find ourselves squarely in the midst of the implicit. Let us consider the following example that illustrates the useful but nonetheless manipulative aspects of deliberate self-disclosure.

(JMN) A divorced woman in her mid-forties is the

patient. She has no children and lives alone. She was born and reared in another city, where her parents still reside. She has a married brother whose home is in a city near her parents. The patient is a highly educated intellectual. She is in a severe crisis as she enters her third year of once-per-week psychotherapy.

She has a high position in a major corporation as administrative assistant to the CEO. That officer is now under major investigation for alleged misuse of his high office. The patient is a person with an impeccable ethical record. She is a person of principle who is well-known for her rectitude. She had done *nothing* wrong. However, her boss has lower standards, the revelations of the investigation may have serious damaging influence upon his corporate career, and the scope of the damage is difficult to predict.

Yet, the CEO himself, a scarred veteran of corporate warfare, seems relatively unruffled by the emerging scandal. My patient, on the other hand, is living in a state of terror. She feels she is going to be pilloried in the press. She fears that her reputation for honor and integrity will be seriously tarnished, if not destroyed. She expects to become a moral pariah and that she will have to retreat to a Midwestern city where she can live out the rest of her life working in the safety of her brother's clothing store. She can hardly sleep or eat, and she retches for a half hour every morning upon rising from her bed. And her mother is now staying with her and sleeping with her. The patient is now on large doses of antidepressant medication. She is able to work, but the cost of remaining in the workplace is very high.

This is a very ironic situation. The culpable party is relatively inured to the threats and blows while the innocent party is reacting as though she has committed a major crime and is awaiting extremely harsh punishment.

Of course, the relevant background is very complex. In some respects, the patient is replicating the terrors of her childhood. Although to the best of her recollection she was treated sensitively and lovingly by her parents, she was a hypersensitive child. If she had to demonstrate learning by a test or a classroom presentation or discussion, she would become extremely anxious, would have insomnia, and would retch and vomit before going to school on that fateful day. Only with the support, reassurance, and firmness of her mother could she manage to go to school and function.

In the early phase of therapy, her extreme sensitivity and guilty vulnerability were evident. Her therapeutic behavior was characterized by sensitive abstraction. This painful guardedness changed sizeably in conjunction with the patient beginning to talk about how she feared to ask me for a favor, to make an inquiry regarding my personal life, or to call me between sessions even when she felt extremely anxious. Extensive talk about these fears and relating them to her childhood fears resulted in some abatement of the anxiety. She then began to make powerful references to my incredible kindness, understanding, and acceptance. We could both talk about how she felt like a vulnerable child. In order that she not feel patronized by me, I would tell her that I also am a big baby, that I also can be plagued with feelings that are very childlike. Therefore, I would say, she need not feel undue shame over sharing such feelings with me. Conversations of this sort occurred in the therapy many months before when the crisis in her office was beginning.

At the height of the crisis, the patient recognized that her terror far exceeded any possible real danger that she might be in and that she was doubtless reliving the dreadful feelings of childhood. Her agony was augmented by shame over being unable to achieve a calmer, more self-possessed state of mind. Therefore, I decided to share some of my history of similar anxiety with her.

I told her how much social terror filled my earlier years. I told her the story of how my parents were politically radical, were very poor, were culturally isolated, and were unnaturalized. I felt myself to be very marginal and dreaded all official institutions and authority figures. The specific fear was that my parents would be arrested and possibly deported.

This was an act of explicit, deliberate self-disclosure. It was subjectively unpleasant, but it felt necessary to me in view of the patient's desperate need for support. I made no effort to render my experience more mature than hers. I told her just what had happened — of the powerful background of fear in my life and of how this kind of fear permeated the entire family, with major consequences for self-esteem.

One purpose of my disclosure was to stimulate closeness and warmth, as though she could gain strength from our huddling together in fear. The patient welcomed this information about me, and no damage to the therapeutic relationship arose from my action. The explicit self-disclosure was necessary to reduce her shame, after which she was more able to focus on her severe anxiety. Shortly after this self-disclosure, she began to express overt sexual feelings toward me for the first time. Such feelings had previously been indirectly evident. The increased sense of mutuality resulting from my self-disclosure now permitted her to share these feelings with me.

5

Interpretation and Intersubjectivity

IS INTERPRETATION AN INTERSUBJECTIVE EVENT?

An interpretation is always an intersubjective event. This is true whether an interpretation is "good" or "bad." A good interpretation means that intense, creative intersubjective resonance is occurring, leading to a richer and more comprehensive consciousness. A bad interpretation fundamentally reflects the therapist's disruptive anxiety over whatever intense intersubjective processes are operating.

The following clinical excerpt presents a good interpretation.

(JMN) The same 30-year-old single female, junior

television executive previously described entered my office for her final analytic session of the week. She began the session by saying, "I had a dream of you last night." In her tone of voice, she seemed also to be saying that this might be an exceptionally important dream because she does not recall dreams of me very often.

> *Dream*: I am entering a room, waiting before entering. It seems to be a party. I have a picture book on chrysanthemums. I want you to inscribe the book. You take it, sign it, and return it to me. I don't know what you've written. I make a comment in which I give a wrong answer. You make a joke out of what I said.
>
> My lover Bill sees you enter the party room, joins you, excitedly saying, "You are Dr. Natterson." And Bill and you enter the room together, in a convivial way. I am not with you, I see you, and I feel humiliated and embarrassed by the events. Bill asks me to come in, but I feel too bad. Also, I tell him that I have to work.
>
> Then I open the book. It has your pat signature — you had written the introduction to the book. It's a cheeky inscription, like, "I know everyone hates chrysanthemums, and so do I." You had a stamp that said that.

The current reality issue that the dream deals with is that the patient's father was to arrive in Los Angeles on the day that she brought the dream to the analysis. As indicated in the dream, she chronically feels hurt and resentful that her father is so much more involved in the life of her functionally impaired brother (as symbolized by the interaction of her analyst and her lover).

This was a dream with strong sexual transference meanings. I was fully aware of them, and I believe the patient was as well. Yet, the interpretive exigencies required focus on the emerging communicative freedom between us. This was the larger context.

Although the dream thus was manifestly about hurt, humiliated, rejected feelings involving me, and although she portrays me in an unpleasant light, other factors pointed to another kind of interpretation. First, the fact that she dreamed of me and remembered and discussed the dream with me suggests greater openness to me. Similarly, casting me in a role akin to some of her important feelings to her father indicated an active, integrating response to interpretations I had been offering recently that emphasized father transference to me. Furthermore, her associations tended to accentuate intimate meanings. For example, chrysanthemums reminded her of Georgia O'Keeffe's erotic drawings of flowers. A quality of great empathic resonance has come to pervade all of our meetings.

Therefore, I interpreted that the dream was essentially paradoxical; although it reveals negative feelings to me in my transference role, the dream very importantly communicates her growing confidence in herself and her consequent greater freedom to express, however subtly, her intense intimate feelings within our relationship. The patient welcomed the interpretation as a perceptive reading of her actual feelings and of the latent implication of the dream.

As support for this interpretation, we have the events of her next analytic session. After the session just discussed, the patient's father arrived for his brief weekend visit. As she had feared, she found him blocked with respect to talking with her about personally important aspects of her life. He seemed to "fill all the space" with himself. She felt increasingly disappointed, hurt, angry, and sad. At one point, he did say he loved her; this remark kept her anchored to him in love, but it did not reduce her acute pain. She was crying throughout this discussion.

From the very beginning of this subsequent session, I experienced acute empathic pain. The hour was extremely poignant, and this was a shared poignancy. I commented to her that I was experiencing her feelings, albeit in an attenuated form. This remark, of course, unleashed more tears and revelations of the pain and hurt she feels in relation to her father's inability to express and receive love to and from her.

This is a good interpretation because, in the best judgment of both patient and analyst, we were having an exceptional experience of analytic intimacy. We were sharing her pain with powerful relevance and resonance. The interpretation correctly picked up the premonitory phenomena of the preceding session and significantly facilitated the full flowering of the feelings in the subsequent session.

DOES AN INTERPRETATION DEAL ONLY WITH THE PATIENT'S PSYCHOLOGICAL LIFE? OR DOES AN INTERPRETATION ALSO EXPRESS THE PSYCHOLOGICAL LIFE OF THE THERAPIST?

Any interpretation, even a bad, defensive, coercive, devaluing, misleading one, invariably expresses a major aspect of the therapist's emotional experience. Only adherence to a ludicrously simplistic black box view of interpretation could provide the logical basis for exclusion of the therapist's psychology from the production, transmission, and verbal form of the interpretation. The interpretation is not only a sharply focused comment on the humanness of the patient but it also expresses the humanness of the therapist, inasmuch as it contains powerful meta-communications of the therapist's subjective life. The therapist's component does not vitiate the interpretation: instead, it is inherent in the interpretation and is a natural component of it.

Let us use the preceding example of a good interpretation to illustrate the answer to this question.

(JMN) My interpretation arose primarily from my basic sense of the meaning of her experience with me at that time. Although she pictured me in the dream as hurting her feelings in several ways, I was deeply impressed by the paradox: I felt quite close to and respectful of her, and I assumed that she was feeling the same toward me. This experience constituted the gist of my interpretation. It is clear that my subjectivity was crucial for the interpretation.

My interpretation was a complex communication that contained various aspects or levels of my subjectivity. These components are not really separable from the patient's subjectivity. It is also impossible to recall fully and to articulate accurately my subjective investment in this interpretation. The following account should be appraised in that light.

When this woman first saw me and told me of leaving her previous therapist because he joined in criticizing her mother harshly, she was also telling me that he was meeting his own erotic needs in a disguised way. I heard this meaning intuitively because I was able to maintain the erotic involvement as a background issue. I very much wanted to be an effective parent who could help her find her own voice and her own self and in that way continue to develop my own identity.

My interest in her as a parent figure has its own interesting basis in my own personal history, but it is sufficient at this point to note that my interpretation to her was inseparable from my own subjective state.

WHO IS CHANGED BY INTERPRETATION?

Since an interpretation is a powerful intimate communication and since it deals with the psychology of both persons, it becomes obvious that both are influenced by the interpretation. The patient changes in response to the interpretation as uttered by the therapist and then changes further in response to his initial response and to the therapist's responses to the patient's response.

The therapist changes as he develops and formulates the interpretation, as he communicates it to the patient, and as he reacts to the patient's response.

If this account suggests a definable beginning and end to an interpretive experience, a correction is needed. The interpretive process is a continuous one during therapy and is ultimately inseparable from the therapeutic process as a whole. The interpretive process is most evident when an interpretation is being expressed, but it is nevertheless continuing even when it is nonevident.

Let us illustrate this question and answer by continuing with a discussion of the same interpretation.

My interpretation of the patient's dream of me obviously was intended to enhance her awareness of the meaning of her dream(s), to increase her awareness of and her capacity to discuss her relationship to me, to clarify continuing problematic aspects of her involvement with the significant people in her life (specifically father and lover), and ultimately to help her achieve a more complete actualization of her self.

These attainments by the patient occur in conjunction with changes in the therapist. My formal analytic wish was to answer the question: "What does the dream mean?" My underlying motive for wanting to provide the answer was to be an effective, facilitating parent to her. This parenting need invariably involves my relationships to my parents and my children, with all the complex meanings of those intimate experiences.

So, as I draw material from my own bank of family memories, I am already undergoing change. The work of formulation of the interpretation maintained the mutative climate. The conveyance of the interpretation, as well as my response to her response, further extended the change in me. The extreme poignancy that I felt in the session after the interpretation showed my powerful response to her response to the interpretation. It was my impression that in this poignant response, I was extending my resolution of the parent-son vicissitudes in my life.

> ### ARE PATIENTS INTERPRETERS OF THE THERAPIST?

The essential reciprocity of the therapeutic relationship, plus its emphasis on interpretation, means that the interpretive fallout will affect both persons in the therapeutic field.

The meta-communicative aspect of therapy includes endless interpretive ideas exchanged between the therapist and the patient. It seems plausible that *all* communication between the patient and therapist is essentially interpretive, just as it is basically a statement of value, and as it is also an expression of the communicator's view of the universe.

(RJF) A potent example of the patient as interpreter to the therapist can be drawn from the analysis of Jane, a 40-year-old woman who, during the course of the analysis, became a prominent real estate executive. From the beginning of the analysis, I always looked forward to seeing Jane each day. My supervisor on the case and I agreed that Jane adopted this pleasing attitude toward me in order to become Daddy's favorite little girl, which she used defensively to ward off strong erotic desires toward a father figure. Our analysis of this dynamic, as well as myriad associated issues, was of considerable benefit to Jane. This interpretive chord eventually allowed her to identify with aggressive qualities common to both her father and myself, and as a result, her career soared.

As her anxiety over aggression diminished and as her need to be Daddy's pleasing little girl gave way to a more mature father–daughter relationship, I realized that I still looked forward to seeing Jane every day. I now became aware that she was a truly happy and serene person.

As our work progressed from paternal issues, the analytic focus turned to her relationship with her mother. The steady analysis of their relationship gradually led me to a global awareness that Jane was in some way "mothering" me. There was clearly a gradient between our happiness quotients in life. My supervisor, in his way, agreed that during the hour I became more optimistic and that in a subliminal way Jane was cheering me up. At the time, this interchange between us was of minimal concern in supervision, and its implications were not deemed important enough to study. However, I am now aware that Jane made the equivalent of endless interpretations to me about my relative (to hers) inability to relax in a maternal relationship because of my fear of being used and thus having to give up my own needs for attention and affection.

I can recall many interchanges in which I would interpret Jane's conflicted anger at her mother. I do not recall the exact precipitants or critical issues that would lead to these interpretations. However, I distinctly remember that Jane would say to me in so many words and in a soft and reassuring voice: "Yes, I thought my mother acted cruelly, but not as bad as you make it sound. How painful it would be to have had a mother like that." I knew that my interpretation had been correct, but that I had gone too far in describing the intensity of affect between mother and child. I can now remember picturing my own mother and our interaction at those times, but only rarely

did I consciously accept Jane's soothing implied interpretation that I had suffered considerable pain in my
relationship with my mother. Most of the time, the
interpretations were given and received at an unconscious,
meta-communicative level.

In the following example, the patient simultaneously
interprets critical issues for himself and for his analyst.
Once again, the process takes place unconsciously. However, we can hypothesize that the patient must certainly be
aware of his contribution to the analyst's insight, and we
could speculate on the significant intersubjective meaning
that helping the analyst possesses for the patient.

(RJF) A male analyst under my supervision was
analyzing Paul, a 42-year-old man who had never allowed
himself to finish college or to hold a steady job. During
this early phase of the analysis, Paul strongly idealized the
analyst. Stormy outbursts surrounding vacations and
other disappointments were brief and did not disrupt the
predominant idealization.

One day, they were analyzing Paul's desire, ap-
proaching a demand, that he be allowed to come for
analytic appointments whenever he needed or wished,
rather than following a preset routine. Paul remarked,
"How can I feel so unimportant on one hand, and so
special on the other," which led to a discussion of feelings
of specialness compensating for feelings of smallness and
inferiority.

Paul continued, "If I'm not special, you won't have
anything to do with me. Ordinary makes me feel like my
father, like the way mother saw him, non-special." He
continued, "How can you love me if I come regularly at set

times? I wouldn't be special!" The analyst felt anxious and confused. In a state of "bewilderment," he began to comment on the idea that Paul was a competent person capable of achieving success and thus gaining love. Paul, on the other hand, kept interjecting that the analyst could never love him if he was ordinary. The analyst's confusion mounted. Finally, Paul said: "I wasn't loved, there was no time for me. I wasn't special to them. Maybe if they had loved me because I was an ordinary little kid, everything would be easier now!" The analyst's tension melted, but he still felt confused. He experienced a wish to see his own analyst, believing that something important in his life was dominating him and clouding his thought.

During our next supervisory hour, we clarified Paul's interpretation of himself and of the analyst. The analyst realized that he was equating acceptance with achievement and that he was confused by his own inability to tolerate the pain of realizing his childhood problem of the same nature. Subsequently, Paul's interpretation became the nidus of the analyst's steady work on these issues in his training analysis.

A similar example is drawn from my own practice. It illustrates the less common occurrence wherein a patient makes an explicit interpretation to the therapist. Such overt interpretations happen with greater frequency than is generally recognized. Unfortunately, too often, patient and therapist joke about such interpretations in awkward, defensive avoidance, thus reducing consciousness of the intersubjective meaning of such events.

(RJF) Robert, a psychologist, was finishing a long analysis with me. He was ambivalently entertaining a commitment to the formal study of psychoanalysis (which he loved), as symbolized by his application to my psycho-analytic institute. One day, our work led to a memory of childhood abuse. Robert sobbed uncontrollably and ago-nizingly while I sat silently. Inwardly, I felt perplexed. On the one hand, I knew Robert was in pain. On the other hand, I was aware of not feeling it. I also felt defensive, for I believed I must be in error for not recognizing what had led up to this traumatic memory. I also wondered guiltily if I had done something to precipitate it.

This was certainly not the first time he re-experienced the pain of his childhood abuse, but it had not previously occurred with such painful intensity. Clearly, I strongly believed I was letting him down in some way. I finally said that there was something wrong, and I said that I sus-pected I had a hand in it. Robert slowly composed himself, which took the remainder of the hour. He indicated that he was upset with me, but too distraught to feel it or discuss it.

In our session on the following day, Robert an-nounced that he experienced my silence as a major rebuff. He described this in detail. At the height of his anger, he accosted me for "your goddam psychoanalytic theories." I wondered aloud if perhaps he was excoriating psychoanal-ysis instead of me personally; for after all, I, Ray Fried-man, had let him down. Robert responded most emphatically: "Yes, you, Ray Friedman, let me wallow in my pain; but what kind of profession doesn't allow you to feel automatically and primarily? It's just wrong!"

There were many layers of meaning to Robert's interpretation, some of which we discussed together over the ensuing months, but most of which I analyzed privately. There was no question in my mind that, by sitting there thinking about his pain instead of making emotional contact, I had failed him and that I had failed him in a hostile way. Once again, I had hurt someone while I was entrusted with the mothering role. The major thrust of Robert's interpretation to me, though, was extremely painful, and its correctness took a long time for me to acknowledge fully. I had placed a theory, or at least the theoretical need to explain, ahead of the human need to respond; I had desperately wanted to deny this professional hideboundness and take the blame totally at a personal level. I could not, however, and over time, Robert's interpretation led me to a new and deeper understanding of the primacy of the intersubjective bond in psychoanalysis.

HOW DOES THE INTERPRETIVE PROCESS OCCUR?

Although the interpretive process is a continuous one throughout therapy, it is nevertheless useful to describe it as having a beginning. Thus, an interpretation arises from the passionate impingement of patient and therapist.

The therapist has an intense subjective experience, which is usually partly conscious and partly unconscious. This experience is characteristically anxiety fraught. Simultaneously, there is some enactment of this subjective state in the therapeutic setting. In order to be able to construct an interpretation, the therapist must be open to his pain and must employ it to transform his own consciousness, so that the anxiety abates. His attention then is able to focus on the patient's subjective state, indispensably informed by the new insights just achieved by the therapist in relation to himself.

Interpretation may be regarded as developing in two stages: the first stage includes the passionate impingement of the two parties and the focus on the therapist's subjectivity. The second stage conforms to the more conventional view of interpretation; the therapist's reflective thought now attends to the patient's subjectivity, and the therapist employs his education and prior experience as aids in the formal construction of the interpretation. For more detailed exposition of this point, see Natterson (1991).

(JMN) In the case of the young woman who had the critical dream in which I inscribe her picture book, it is relatively easy to illustrate the two-stage process of interpretation formation.

The patient was very much preoccupied with the feeling of being deprived of attention and affirmation by her parents, especially her father. I brought to the moment my own lifelong search for a more uninhibited, involved father. It was the dynamic encounter of these two sets of closely related needs that constituted the first stage of interpretation formation.

Then began the second stage of interpretation building. Although she had negative feelings toward me in the dream, I was unable to contact these negative emotions in her. Instead, on the basis of the shared dynamics cited above, I felt our warmth and closeness to one another. From this I could resolve the paradox of a dream that seems to express negative feelings to me but that felt experientially positive: the negative feelings belong to her father, but due to guilt, she is obliged to displace them to me. However, the act of sharing the negative feelings with me expresses her loving and trusting feelings toward me.

I engaged in the above reflective thought and could then formulate and deliver the interpretation.

6

Intersubjectivity and the Therapist's Manifest Behavior

It is a virtual truism that no two therapists are alike, even if their theoretical orientations are identical; hence, even a reasonably complex answer to this question may be very incomplete and therefore ambiguous. With this strong caveat, the following answers are offered.

The differences between an intersubjective therapist and a conventional therapist are fundamentally conceptual and may not be directly expressed in overt behavior. Some therapists are more talkative and expressive than others. Some are more laconic and less animated. These differences are often based on temperament and may have little to do with theoretical orientation.

The behavioral effects of an intersubjective orientation have to be looked for in a more holistic way. For example, the intersubjectivist examines his ongoing subjective experience in a special way: he not only considers his subjectivity as *reacting* but also as *initiating*. Thus, he considers two ongoing narratives — the patient's and his own — simultaneously, how they converge and diverge, and how each party's subjective experience shapes and is shaped by the other's. This constitutes a different way of listening and participating. The interpretive dialogue therefore is more ambiguous and less systematic, in contrast to the more linear character of a more conventional therapeutic dialogue. However, this difference may not be apparent at any cross-sectional moment of the therapeutic dialogue. It would be more evident if one studies or examines a larger segment of a therapy.

Not only is the interactional quality different, as just described, but also the direction or course of therapy is different. A greater explicit emphasis on the quality and transformation of consciousness of both participants characterizes intersubjectively informed therapy, whereas a conventionally based therapy tends to place more emphasis only on the process of uncovering the patient's "truths." Thus, the content of the dialogue solidly displays these differences.

The following example is drawn from a psychotherapy consultation.

(JMN) A sensitive and well-trained therapist was

discussing a case with me, and as she presented a session, she stated emphatically, "I think I may have made a real mistake here." She explained that as she listened to her patient, her eyes "moistened with tears." She said that in her own previous, unsuccessful therapy, her female therapist would often have tearful responses and that the effect was antitherapeutic. Similarly, the supervisee's mother has always had overly pained responses, which would cause the supervisee to withdraw, regretting that she shared any problem with her mother.

I commented that it sounded to me as though she experienced her mother as responding excessively to her, thereby stealing her psychological space from her. The supervisee said that this is exactly how she feels whenever her mother does this.

This supervisee who reported her tearfulness to me told me that the patient is an Asian in her mid-thirties who has recently started therapy. She is a tiny woman who in the initial sessions told of an isolated life, revealed much paranoid thinking, and showed no affect. In this session, however, she wept and expressed how unhappy her life feels. It was in the midst of these sentiments that the therapist found herself near tears.

I had no doubt of the intersubjective significance of her tears. The patient was suffering, and the therapist responded with pain that was registered in her eyes. Yet, her initial cognitive response was intersubjectively naive. That is, she felt anxious on the basis that she was doing something wrong and should therefore stifle the tears.

As we discussed the events that had occurred with her patient and how they linked up to her feelings to her mother and her own previous therapist, she began to realize that the meaning of tearfulness cannot be concretized or reduced to a unitary meaning of the kind that she had experienced with her mother and her therapist. Her tears arose in the context of the patient beginning to share emotions with her, and her responsive tearfulness was a supporting, acknowledging, facilitating expression of her resonant involvement. Her tears told the patient that she, the therapist, could appreciate the patient's desperation. Additionally, the therapist's tears acknowledged the patient's separateness while at the same time providing intimate sharing and support. This was the therapist's thwarted desire toward her own mother. The therapist now had a refined recognition that she brought this dynamic to the encounter with the patient. This dynamic helped initiate the patient's expression of her suffering.

So the therapist had now employed her tearfulness as the vehicle that led her to a clearer understanding of her own psychological participation (her narrative) with the patient. In turn, she could now more fluently empathize with and comprehend her patient's own struggle to secure and develop her own life space. In summary, the therapist first conceptualized an event in therapy with intersubjective naivete. However, by questioning and exploring her initial view, she achieved an intersubjectively informed position.

The intersubjective perspective enabled the therapist to reflect on her tearfulness and especially upon what attitudes and needs she brought to the therapeutic encounter, as well as how they helped shape the therapeutic process. Questions of technique thus became secondary.

WOULD THE BEHAVIOR OF AN
INTERSUBJECTIVE THERAPIST APPEAR
THE SAME AS OR DIFFERENT FROM
THAT OF A CONVENTIONAL THERAPIST
TO AN INTERESTED THIRD PARTY?

The Heisenberg principle has eliminated the proverbial Man from Mars. So, an interested third party cannot also be a disinterested third party. From an intersubjective standpoint, in his act of observing he will also be influencing the transaction. His influence will be facilitating or obstructing, depending upon his degree of openness to an intersubjective analysis. But, to reiterate, he cannot be a pure observer.

So, a third party's observation will be influenced by the values, memories, and prejudices with which he encounters the therapeutic events.

But what about the therapeutic emanations themselves? Intersubjective therapy rests on the inseparability of the two involved subjectivities. The boundaries between the two will be fluid, supple, permeable, and, at times, non-evident. Not so in a conventional therapy, in which the very emphasis on clarifying boundaries may engender more of an impression of separateness between the two parties.

Overall, a conventional therapy may convey to an observer a greater impression of direction toward, proximity to, or distance from a goal. This helps establish a crisper definition of therapist and of patient. In contrast, an intersubjective therapy may momentarily obscure the role differences between therapist and patient. However, these differences are maintained in intersubjective therapy, even though they are less evident. For instance, this blurring would be evident when therapy is in a state of creative flux and the therapist surrenders to the process. The profound intersubjective experience momentarily blurs the therapist's consciousness of the clear distinction between patient and therapist roles. Although powerful, this state can be very subtle, and the naive observer might be rendered confused and anxious or might be oblivious to its occurrence.

This example illustrates how the intensity of the intersubjective process blurs boundaries between the two parties, even as it is facilitating greater differentiation.

(JMN) A 65-year-old divorced attorney has a significant relationship with a divorced woman who lives in another city. They were sweethearts in high school, and then they drifted apart. They are now lovers and seriously considering marriage. She has been ready for marriage, but he is quite ambivalent.

He has now returned to therapy after a delightful two-week holiday with her in her home city. In the therapy, he agonizes over the decision. When he is with her, he enjoys her very much and feels that he loves her. However, when he returns to his Los Angeles home, he begins to have doubts.

His pain of indecision seems to flow from him into me. As he squirms and grimaces in his struggle with his options, I feel tense and blocked within myself. I painfully ask myself what the right decision is for him, and I begin to think of my own anguish over making important life decisions. This problem of mine has abated over the years, so that I am genuinely dismayed at how little confidence this patient has in himself. Yet, I am in contact with my own earlier severe indecisiveness so that I can feel that this patient's painful dilemma is almost my own. At such moments, the clear role distinctions between him and me have virtually dissolved. I can perceive that my earlier self-problem was crucial to my inability to make important decisions. This realization helps me be clear with myself and with him that our most urgent task is the facilitation of his self-defining and self-affirming capabilities so that he can make reasonable decisions and stay with them. Unfortunately, at present and throughout his life, he has collapsed his own identity into that of some other authoritative person.

In the therapy, he and I have achieved important understanding of the dynamics of his developmental family that obstructed healthy self-esteem and self-definition and consequently impaired his decision-making capabilities.

My view is that, during the sessions, when he and I feel bonded through his pain, it is as though our shared suffering is a crucible in which new aspects of his self are formed. The unity of him and me is both transient and very therapeutic.

DOES AN INTERSUBJECTIVE THERAPIST BEHAVE INDISTINGUISHABLY FROM THE PATIENT?

An intersubjective orientation in psychotherapy above all emphasizes oneness with differences. The power of therapeutic intimacy increases markedly through the voluntary relinquishing of boundaries between the principals, as well as through the consequent subordination of attention to the explicit role differences of the two parties.

The paradox in this is that the result of this therapeutic fusion is a fundamental strengthening of each individual, with an attendant increased understanding by therapist and by patient of their respective roles in the therapeutic situation.

Perhaps an intersubjectivist is less preoccupied with the formalities of therapy than a conventional therapist would be. In this way, it might be more difficult to distinguish patient from therapist. In other ways, however, the therapist and patient would be readily distinguished from one another. The patient would certainly continue to be the more talkative one and also would be the reporter and discusser of pain, whereas the therapist, although also feeling the pain, would tend to talk more evaluatively and interpretively, as in any therapy. The following case illustrates some of these points.

(JMN) A poet-actor in his late forties had recently relinquished alcohol and had become increasingly anxious and irritable. He entered therapy with me because he wished to understand himself better and to achieve more inner tranquility.

The patient had been in psychotherapy several years earlier, and he had found it very helpful. On beginning with me, he experienced some initial unease because of my informal manner, which contrasted starkly with the style of his previous therapist. Nevertheless, we developed a productive therapeutic dialogue quite rapidly, with an equivalent and gratifying degree of symptom reduction.

As time passed, we both observed that our manifest interactions were changing. There continued to be many periods in which we worked in traditional ways with dreams, problematic relations with family members, difficulties in work activities, and other typical therapeutic preoccupations. Yet, another kind of shared experience developed.

These were periods of shared creative excitement. We would compare mental notes, and in doing so, we were able to share our similar experiences of nonlinear, ambiguous consciousness. In these periods of therapy, unusual images, often of a spatial nature, would be part of each of our consciousnesses. Out of this chaotic, unorganized state of consciousness, the patient would emerge with an enhanced sense of self. His relational understanding of this interaction is that he is having a joyous collaboration experience that helps liberate him from the oppressive controls he developed out of his relationship with his hysterical mother.

When we first realized that periods of intense creative flux were occurring, we felt as though they were moments of fortunate happenstance. However, we quickly became aware that these were, in fact, inexorable developments arising from the conjoining of our shared delight in the unconventional aspects of human consciousness.

Of special interest is the fact that many periods of this therapy were quite like so many other therapies, in form and content. It should be evident that this was an intersubjectively informed therapy that often seemed quite conventional, and at other times, quite unconventional.

> # DOES THE INTERSUBJECTIVE
> # THERAPIST DISCLOSE ALL HIS
> # ASSOCIATIONS AND FEELINGS AS THE
> # PATIENT TENDS TO DO?

Simply put, *no*.

Here we refer to explicit, deliberate verbal disclosure by the therapist. Such behavior would obviously result in cacophonous competition between patient and therapist. The damaging effect of such indiscriminate verbalization by the therapist would be a stifling invasion of the patient's life space, a deflection from the thoughts and feelings in which the patient had been immersed, and anger and depression in the patient arising from the damaging behavior of the therapist.

The notion of the indiscriminately talkative therapist probably reflects an unconscious resistance by those who hold this notion to the powerful implications of the intersubjective position. The patient who has need and the therapist who offers help are facts of life. The application of intersubjective theory to psychotherapy is an effort to make therapy more understandable and effective. There is no intention to render therapist indistinguishable from patient by suggesting that the therapist reveal all his thoughts and feelings just as the patient does.

On the other hand, therapists should be judiciously self-revealing—on selected occasions. One of us (JMN) has had the following experience of feeling emotional pain in his upper abdomen. He has found that this usually reflects a sad or depressed feeling in the patient. Sometimes, when he has this abdominal sensation, he simply asks the patient if he is feeling sad. At other times, he reveals that he is having this abdominal experience, that it usually indicates sadness in the patient, and is that the case now? He offers this self-disclosing component when he feels that the patient needs the support of knowing that the therapist is responding to and sharing his pain.

In the following example, the therapist knowingly and deliberately keeps his thoughts to himself (such moments seem to occur multiple times in every therapeutic session).

(JMN) A 45-year-old Latino woman is in the midst of another typical session. She is depressed and frustrated over her life. She is unhappy with her husband; she feels guilty, deprived, and helpless over the estrangement from her only sibling; and she feels limited in a broader sense because of a lack of career success. She also expresses the shame she felt in adolescence over her parents' depreciated minority status, as she began mingling for the first time with Anglo students.

As she speaks, I have various thoughts, none of which I express to her at the time. My least accepting thought is that she complains a great deal—too much—about her life, that complaining is her way of life. I felt that this unflattering perception of the patient was potentially useful, but that its usefulness would be destroyed if I conveyed it to her in this preliminary and rather crude form. Instead, I became aware that some immature complaining tendencies of my own were activated, as well as some of my own adolescent shame over my own parents. Later in the session, I was able to interpret with some effectiveness that the patient is saddled with a great deal of ambivalence toward her parents. I also indicated that she has a similar potential for such feelings of love and hate toward me, feelings that she characteristically does not recognize.

This represents a sequence of cognitive (and emotional) events in me. Had I needed to verbalize them, I would probably have aborted my own process of developing the interpretation, and we would have been diverted into some other discussion. Yet, this was an intersubjectively informed series of thoughts and acts on my part: my subjectivity conjoined hers, and a productive session resulted.

(JMN) Here is another example of a case in which I am a "quiet" therapist. The patient is a short, intellectual woman in her early fifties. She typically sits quietly in my waiting room, waiting for me to enter the room and greet her. Her response is usually a silent nod of acknowledgment, as she enters my office and lies on the couch without comment. She usually begins the session by stating that she feels good or bad and then commences to speak about the circumstances that produce her good or bad feelings. Her voice is soft and steady. Although her manner is undramatic, I often think of her as someone who exemplifies the saying, "Still waters run deep."

My typical response is a subdued, puzzled receptivity. It would seem quite incongruous for me to speak out now. I feel much more like an information gatherer than an information provider. My intervention seems not to be welcome at this time, and I do not feel a desire or inspiration to enter the conversational field. She wants to talk, and she wants to do so in her way, without interference. Usually, as the session goes on, things warm up, and a bilateral conversation may develop. Such is not always the case, however. Frequently, my verbal activity is limited to some questions and/or an interpretation.

I do not feel angry or deprived, although I am aware that she and I could have a more reciprocal verbal exchange. Instead, I identify with her, thinking of how much of my emotional and fantasy life I have kept to myself. I remember how she has always felt excluded from the charmed circle of her mother and older siblings. I realize that, in some way, she and I are re-enacting the old pattern of exclusion, although it is not clear who is the excluded one.

This has always been considered by both of us to be a very productive analytic experience. The laconic mode of verbal interaction typifies the analytic style that we have developed, but it does not make a greater or lesser therapeutic experience.

This example shows how quietness in a therapist may be an integral part of a therapeutic process, expressing characterological and historical features of the patient. This same quietness partakes of potentials for quietness in the therapist. It becomes a therapeutic process that moves forward in a quiet way. But this, of course, is not the only kind of situation in which a therapist becomes quiet.

I can recall situations in which I have been quiet because of a feeling that anything I might say would elicit the patient's rage. It is also common for me to be quiet when I can make no sense of what a patient is saying (or not saying), and my quietness is a measure of the resistance in the patient.

> # WHY IS IT HAZARDOUS TO JUDGE THE APPROPRIATENESS OF A THERAPIST'S BEHAVIOR ACCORDING TO WHETHER HE IS LACONIC OR LOQUACIOUS?

Being silent or speaking results from a choice made by the therapist. The exceptions to this statement are those conditions in which some inner pressure, usually anxiety, impels the therapist to talk, in relative disregard for the immediate dialogical requirements, or when a powerful inhibiting force—also usually anxiety—creates an insurmountable obstacle for the therapist who falls silent, which is also not an appropriate response to the therapy's communicative requirements.

Under favorable conditions, the intersubjective therapist resonates with the patient and with his own different zones of consciousness. Therefore, he has greater choice of whether, how, and what to speak.

The conventionally oriented therapist is more likely to attempt to objectify his verbal behavior according to a theoretical a priori assumption. For example, a conventional therapist might insist that any interpretation other than a transference interpretation is an unwarranted and damaging entry by the therapist into the field of discourse, which is purely the patient's. This assumption is based upon a one-person theory of neurosis and of cure. Such an assumption excludes intersubjective considerations and tends to reduce the potential for therapist flexibility.

WHAT FACTORS INDUCE QUIETNESS IN A THERAPIST?

A quiet therapist therefore may be neurotically inhibited, may be in a state of profound resonance with the patient, or may be adhering to a conventional rule that essentially forbids most verbal communication with the patient. It is probable that he is silent on the basis of intuitive intersubjective attunement, yet his silence may be rationalized on the basis of conventional strictures, and it may also be laced with neurotic elements.

WHAT FACTORS PRODUCE TALKATIVENESS IN A THERAPIST?

A talkative therapist may be neurotically driven to express, to make verbal contact. Talkativeness is a kind of acting out in that its real meaning is not understood, and it does relieve anxiety. Or a talkative therapist may have found a theoretical position that emphasizes "honesty" and the total abandonment of any authoritarian trappings.

Or in a certain psychotherapeutic situation, the therapist may perceive a patient's need to be conversationally held or stimulated, and the therapist may respond by increasing the intensity and frequency of his remarks. Again, it should be remembered that in any circumstance, the therapist's own view of the world is at work. That is, he is not simply responding objectively to a need of the patient, but his own subjectivity is continuously involved.

The same previously mentioned poet-actor in his late forties has a characteristic manner of initiating the session. With him, I am a talkative therapist.

The patient is usually a few minutes early, and when I come to greet him, he is sitting forward in his chair, reading a magazine. He typically bounces out of his chair to greet me — with a warm hello and a hearty handshake. He also brings two plastic containers of exotic coffee, one for him and one for me. By the time we cross the threshold of my office, we are usually already engaged in conversation.

As I reflect on my work with this patient, I realize that he and I share a similar view of the therapeutic universe. We both extend eagerly to relate, to know the other, and each of us augments this shared desire to know the mystery of the other. For him and me, it becomes inevitable that we become a loquacious pair.

And what do we talk about? He, like any highly motivated patient, talks about his feelings and fantasies, about his childhood, about his marriage and family, about his career, and about the therapeutic relationship. On the other hand, my verbalizations do not deal with my same categories of life. Rather, I talk about how I experience him and the feelings and perceptions that arise in relation to our shared experience. So here is an example that illustrates two additional points. First, a therapist who is relatively expressive and spontaneous does not necessarily become formally self-disclosing; second, the spirit of friendship and equality that pervades our relationship does not abolish the inevitable asymmetry of a therapeutic relationship or interfere with the expression of negative transference.

Another dimension of this friendly, informal therapeutic atmosphere consists of the patient's freedom, even readiness, to regress *because of the spirit of equality*. He knows that he is being neither devalued nor patronized. Therefore, he searches for the childish, the immature, in his reactions and thoughts. He discusses them enthusiastically, and he has no need to engage in defensive, self-protective euphemizing.

The general principle here is that for patients who can achieve a strong sense of trust and affection, the therapist's spontaneous and informal participation facilitates the so-called therapeutic split in the ego, whereby the patient can experience valuable therapeutic regression while maintaining an effective observing ego.

Obviously, not all patients can readily develop the requisite level of trust for the achievement of this productive therapeutic circumstance. The intersubjectively sophisticated therapist, who attends to his fantasy interaction with the patient, can best know how or whether to move with the patient into a mode of overt spontaneity.

One final note. Some patients achieve powerful therapeutic regression when the therapist is more restrained and less spontaneous. Yet, when this condition prevails, it also should arise out of the therapist's access to his own subjective experience of this patient.

7

Intersubjectivity: Present versus Past

DOES INTERSUBJECTIVITY MEAN THAT
ONLY THE IMMEDIATE
THERAPIST–PATIENT TRANSACTIONS
ARE RELEVANT IN PSYCHOTHERAPY?

Definitely not! Intersubjectivity means that all factors contributing to human subjectivity must be understood and acknowledged. This means that everything contributing to consciousness has importance. Personal history thus remains highly relevant.

The term *historical consciousness* applies here. An individual's historical consciousness is a record of all his previous subjective experiences in life. It obviously in-

cludes his memories, values, traditional beliefs, prejudices, and other similar qualities of consciousness that he
has developed through his various intimate and social
relationships (including his formal education).

Limitation of intersubjectivity's meaning to the immediate, cross-sectional experience with another person is
to render it virtually synonymous with interaction, thus
depriving it of its powerful historical dimensions, which
are always operative.

Yet, this affirmation of historicity need not require a
devaluation or de-emphasis of the primary mediating role
of the here-and-now therapeutic transactions. To para-
phrase a popular environmentalist slogan ("Think glo-
bally, act locally"), an intersubjectivist's motto could be,
"Think historically, act currently."

An obvious contradiction between the current and the
historical should not lead the therapist to believe that he or
she must choose between them. Instead, he or she should
welcome the contradiction as a mark of the inevitably
limited nature of his or her understanding, and he or she
should experience it as a kind of tonic, as a stimulus to
study in the gray area where the past and the present
interact creatively. The following case demonstrates the
importance of the current therapeutic process in the
reconstruction and utilization of the patient's past.

(JMN) A man in his mid-forties behaves as though he
is continuously, breathlessly harassed. He leads his life in
a state of sustained anxiety over whether he has met the
expectations of everyone else in his environment. This
includes his wife, his children, and me.

A constructivist perspective enables us to say that,

together, he and I have indeed created some very important meanings. First of all, we have jointly created a climate of trust in which he can recognize his incessant worry over meeting his obligations to the various significant figures in his life world. In fact, we have also erected that same kind of worry in the therapeutic relationship. Second, we have constructed a shared, informal version of him: much anxiety and obsessive self-doubt. These concepts of himself had not existed consciously before our work.

He and I have been working very conscientiously on these neurotic manifestations in his important current life relationships — including our relationship. The experience that he and I share is intersubjectively intense. He goes from guilty crisis to guilty crisis in his life. This pattern resonates with my own tendencies. In my case, the personal experiences of feeling beholden to almost everyone are couched largely in the memories of past relationships: parents, siblings, teachers, neighbors, and others. In contrast, the patient rarely brings up early life experiences in a spontaneous way. Yet, I believe my regular counterpart past associations have indicated that, subtextually, I have been invoking the past. And, with increasing frequency, he is now turning to relational events in childhood in which he experienced a horror of being selfish or remiss.

These newly emerging past associations are heavily laden with affect and have obvious relevance to the current patterns of behavior that bedevil him. These past memories have arisen in an eruptive manner and have not been coaxed out of him by any conscious efforts of mine to lead him by making reconstructive comments. In fact, when I have made such efforts, they have invariably failed.

Yet, he and I know that I do something that helps elicit aspects of his past that unite with events in the present. Shortly after starting to work with me, he reported to me that in conversation with a friend, he had described his therapy thusly: "I go into the office and sit down. Then, he does something, and these strange and wonderful thoughts start coming out of me." The mutative influence from me comes precisely from my parallel associations, in which I match his current crises with past similar ones from my own life. Out of this admixture of past and present, his overt and mine subtextual, emerges the changed state of consciousness that then enable him to recall past crucial events.

This therapeutic process shows how past and present are powerful temporal polarities in intersubjective therapy.

Some believe that the constructivist perspective refers only to the immediate therapist–patient transactions. In our view, the constructivist perspective is necessarily relative. It does have a broad scope inasmuch as it entails both contemporary transformational influence, as well as early life developmental relevance.

Perhaps the ultimate therapist should have a dual attentiveness; that is, at any given moment, he is immersed in the transaction as he and the patient are transforming their own and each other's consciousness through the relationship and the dialogue. At the same time, the therapist maintains his historical consciousness — of both the patient and himself. Contradiction between the past and the present generates a creative tension, as well as a lubricating resonance that facilitates an increasing consciousness of both sectors of experiences.

Self-consciousness cannot exist without an appreciation of the consciousness of others. It is this interpenetration of the consciousness of different individuals that constitutes the basis of intersubjectivity.

Working with dreams can provide marvelous illustrations of a constructivist approach that also includes sufficient appreciation of preformed historical contributions by both patient and therapist. The dream that follows is a typical example of how a flexible constructivism can be applied to a dream.

> (JMN)
> *Dream*: I am in a house. There is a young guy with short hair; he has an all-American look and is looking for food. I am calling the guy a deviate.
> Then I go to the bathroom. I am kissing a young woman between her legs; I am having sex with her. I seem to recognize her. At the same time, the young guy is in another room with people.
> Then I am also in the other room, flat on my back. The guy has one hand pressing down on my chest. He is killing me.

The dreamer is a man in his middle fifties, a general practitioner, who for many months has suffered severe financial reverses. In the same period he has also been almost solely preoccupied with extremely complex and expensive malpractice litigation.

He reported the dream at the beginning of the session and then tried to offer associations to it. He had no idea who the "young guy" was. He enjoyed the sexual part of the dream, and he thought of how his wife has no interest in sex. Because of his wife's indifference, he said that he finds himself thinking sexually about other women. He had a strong feeling that the guy pressing on his chest, trying to kill him, is the very aggressive attorney for his adversary.

I had my own impressions of the dream, some of which I shared with the patient later in the session. First of all, I was reminded of the patient's all-American look, and I therefore thought the "young guy" might represent the patient. I have always been impressed by the patient's narcissistic self-indulgence and on numerous occasions have speculated silently about its ultimate implications for the patient's psychological life. An interesting aspect of this intensive treatment situation is that his chronic difficulty in articulating his deeper psychological issues has persisted even as his dream life has become abundantly available. Similarly, a shared sense of intimacy has steadily grown within our relationship.

This set of therapeutic conditions has required that I make many significant interpretations in silence, trusting that in some subtextual or metacommunicative way the unstated interpretations would have a therapeutic effect. Furthermore, the patient's resistance to insight seemed to stimulate in me a silent dialogue in which one of my "voices" speaks for me and the other "voice" speaks for the patient. His demeanor toward me is consistently friendly and respectful, even bordering on the soft and submissive. His struggle with his invasive, sadistic father merges with my lifelong conflict with my own unavailable, passive–aggressive father. My early search for fathering and my feminine identification constitute sustained foci in my work with this patient.

All the above converged in my consciousness to create the interpretation, which I held silently within me, that the dream expressed a narcissistic homoerotic preoccupation that derived from his relationship to his father, to me, and to his main adversaries in his current legal and financial battles.

Although he is not yet ready to understand the most powerful psychodynamic themes of his dreams, he is moving slowly but surely in that direction. His narcissistic defenses have blocked his full achievement of selfhood. Yet, he has an intuitive appreciation of the need to achieve a more authentic self. He counts on my guidance toward attaining that goal.

In connection with this dream, I asked him for the first time in our several years of therapeutic engagement about homosexual matters in his life. He responded that he recalls no homosexual experience or desire in his life. I concluded that it was still premature to share my thoughts about unconscious, narcissistic, sadomasochistic, homoerotic preoccupations with him. However, I do believe that by asking the question about homosexuality, I was overtly introducing the subject into the dialogue, and I probably conveyed my belief that this is the issue on which we are currently working.

His narcissism is eroding gradually. He tells me intermittently that he has become much more sensitive to other people's pain, worry, and problems than he was before his therapy. In the past, he was arrogant and insensitive or submissive and compliant. His sense of autonomy is steadily growing. I believe this dream will become a landmark in his journey toward achieving a true selfhood.

To provide an example supporting the constructivist position, I have given some impressions of how he and I interact to transform his consciousness and thereby construct a newer, more valid self. Yet, in the example, I strive to demonstrate that this construction of new subjective meanings does not just occur out of subjective thin air. That is, it is not utterly a here-and-now event. Instead, each of us brings his own personal past, his currently constituted self to the constructive encounter.

Donnel Stern (1991), relying heavily on H. G. Gadamer (1962, 1966, 1967, 1975), emphasizes that each therapeutic participant brings his own assemblage of prejudices to the encounter. The therapeutic experience transforms the prejudices of both therapist and patient. Therefore, the patient, as well as the therapist, brings many psychologically formed elements to the therapy: ordinary memories, traumatic memories, values, prejudices, and transference potentials. These formed elements enjoy greater or lesser degrees of consciousness, and they do find a place in the total therapeutic transaction. They exist before the therapy, although when they become more conscious as a result of therapy, one may think of them as being relatively constructed in the therapy.

Probably, the most clearly constructed aspects of therapy are the therapeutic dialogue itself and the relationship to oneself and other (patient and therapist). Out of this new relationship and its progressive evolution are also constructed the new emotional conditions that permit the further experience in consciousness and dialogue of the variety of formed psychological elements to which we have just referred.

> ## IS THE INDIVIDUAL PAST OF THE PATIENT AND OF THE THERAPIST A CRUCIAL COMPONENT OF THE INTERSUBJECTIVE PROCESS?

We began to answer this question in the preceding comments. The reply is a definite *yes*! Whether history is acknowledged or not, it is always *present* and always important. Remember, *any* aspect of our immediate conscious experience is *always* interactive with our entire personal history.

The therapeutic moment is constituted by the reciprocal impingement of two people's rich and complex personal histories. Often, certain historical moments become obvious as playing a crucial role in shaping the current moment. These are discussed next.

> ## TRANSFERENCE: SHOULD WE REGARD IT AS THE HISTORICAL DIMENSION OF THE PATIENT'S SUBJECTIVITY?

Everyone knows what *transference* means, yet no one knows exactly and irrefutably what it denotes, let alone what it connotes. Freud coined the term, meaning the phenomenon of the past living in the present, usually in disguise. So long as psychoanalysis remained a one-person psychology, this definition was reasonably clear and sufficient. However, in the recent past, as psychoanalysis has moved conceptually to becoming a two-person psychology, it became increasingly difficult to identify the more or less pure recurrence of past desire, conflict, and defense in the current analytic relationship. Now, the term transference means an amalgam of the patient's response to the therapeutic reality, the therapist's response to the therapeutic reality, and the influence of past experience on the immediate response of both patient and therapist. In the case of the therapist, this is, of course, often called *countertransference*.

No sharp line can ever be drawn between the part of the patient's experience that is related only to the present and that which derives solely from the past. In fact, the notion of such exclusivity is a fictive assumption.

The total response of the therapeutic participants should be called *subjectivity*. If one wishes, then, the historical dimension of that total subjectivity can be labeled transference. It is important to realize, however, that no therapeutic experience is ever completely transferential or nontransferential. Every such experience is always an amalgam of past and present. The historical dimension may become more conscious (it usually does in therapy), and it may become otherwise transformed. Yet, it can never be eliminated, because it is a fundamental component of our subjectivity.

Here, we are obviously making transference a subordinate component of the complete subjective experience. Paradoxically, doing so enhances the forceful role of historical factors by liberating them from the previous dominance of a confining definition of transference.

8

Clinical Concepts Relevant to Intersubjectivity

HOW DOES *UNCONSCIOUS GUILT* FIT INTO AN INTERSUBJECTIVE PERSPECTIVE?

The term *unconscious guilt* is a cornerstone of psychoanalysis. It embodies various crucial analytic concepts: unconscious psychological processes, conflict with a loved one, a suffering response to the conflict, and unforeseeable consequences (usually harmful) of this painful conflict.

Unconscious guilt originates in an intersubjective context. Let us say that the conflict exists in the relationship of son and father. The roots, growth, and resolution all involve the bilateral subjective contribution of both son and father. That is, both create and both are influenced by the total experience of the conflict. The particular kind of father and the particular kind of son determine the characteristics of the whole course of the unconscious guilt in the specific individual. It may be true that the first cause of unconscious guilt is biological, with the maleness of the son colliding with the maleness of the father. Yet, the collision is mutually induced and is in that sense intersubjective. Both parties become subjectively intertwined along this guilty axis.

The relationship of son and father evolves, with the unconscious guilt of each toward the other continuously shaping the relationship in powerful ways. The same conditions obtain in later relationships, in which the unconscious guilt of each party is an active, bilateral, shaping component. In therapy, the unconscious guilt of both patient and therapist is operating continuously — with varying levels of intensity and obviousness. The guilt in the patient may result in repression or in any number of other defensive operations whereby the unconscious guilt acts to deprive the patient of the effective knowledge of his own psychological truths.

Sadomasochistic impasses or crises occur frequently within the therapeutic relationship. As is well known, unconscious guilt in a patient often induces a need for punishment or suffering. A therapist who shares unconscious guilt may find such a patient a suitable target for the externalization of his own guilt and may then act out against the patient the hostility (sadism) that helped originally to produce the unconscious guilt. Similarly, the patient may externalize his or her sadistic tendencies onto the therapist.

Therapeutic situations of chronic submission by the patient to the dominance of the therapist may well reflect the above dynamics. This pernicious intersubjective situation persists until a greater consciousness is achieved by both parties. Such reciprocal awareness enables patient and therapist to recognize the desires that underlay the guilt that produced the sadomasochism. In turn, this change results in a more productive intersubjective encounter, wherein the basic attitudes of patient and therapist toward one another become more accessible to the therapeutic dialogue.

IS *IDENTIFICATION* CENTRAL TO THE INTERSUBJECTIVE PROCESS?

We deliberately define *identification* in loose, general terms. We do not attempt to render fine distinctions between identification and other terms such as introjection, internalization, and incorporation.

As is well known, identification occurs both consciously and unconsciously. Our primary point is that, in the therapeutic situation, identification does not occur without the participation of both the therapist and patient. This mutuality renders the event intersubjective.

Although we do not focus particularly on the term identification in our clinical thinking, it is one of the concepts most apposite to our work. This is so because identify means "I am like you" or even "I am you." It is the readiness of each party in the therapeutic transaction to relinquish his or her clear sense of separateness and difference from the other party that is crucial for a therapeutic process to occur. This has always been true, even in the past, when therapists thought that they should and could be quite separate and distinct from their patients and that such a stance was quite compatible with therapeutic progress. In therapy, each party wants and needs the other party to identify with him or her, and each wants and needs to identify with the other.

At times this sense of identification or sameness or likeness between the two parties is felt intensely, and at other times the tendency is subordinated and nonevident. Yet, it is operative at all times in therapy, or the therapy ceases. And, remember, it is always occurring in both therapist and patient. Without identification and its attendant blurring of boundaries, no therapy occurs.

Therapy, like all relationships, is a continuously interactive process. It is no longer supportable to assume that a patient can identify unilaterally with a therapist, that a patient can do so entirely unbidden by the therapist, and that the seeming detachment of the therapist's commentary on the patient's identification is anything but illusory.

IS *EMPATHY* AN INEVITABLE OUTCOME
OF INTERSUBJECTIVELY INFORMED
THERAPY?

Empathy has enjoyed a spectacular prominence in the current era of psychotherapy. At times, it even seems to be the private preserve of self psychology. It is our impression, possibly unfair, that self psychology treats empathy as a specific psychotherapeutic attitudinal skill that is an indispensable precedent to an effective psychotherapeutic process. Such a concept tends to objectify or reify the phenomenon of empathy.

Rather, empathy seems to be an artificial, but nonetheless useful, concept that somewhat precariously describes qualities of transaction that develop whenever a rich and productive intersubjective engagement is achieved. Although there can be some usefulness to talking about the degree of empathy or the kind of empathy in a given situation, such accounts also partake of the objectification of empathy, which is a fundamental impossibility. This is a reason we prefer to talk adjectivally as in empathic or empathizing. Thus, like Schafer (1976), we minimize use of the noun empathy and we thereby reduce the reifying hazard.

The patient feels understood when the therapist feels understanding. This understanding by the therapist is passionate, as well as compassionate. In such a circumstance, the therapist invariably is in touch with his own emotional needs and conflicts as well as with those of the patient. It seems probable that, in some less tutored way, counterpart events are occurring in the patient. This would be an instance of creative flux, either quiet or noisy, in which there is boundaryless intermingling of the two selves. In this area of porous, amorphous interface, each self is partially confused with the other, so that the distinction between understanding oneself and understanding the other is transiently lost. This intermingling is a necessity for genuine and therapeutically effective empathic influence. The empathic dimension of therapy therefore should be conceived as emerging from both parties.

Empathic offerings and responses are often indistinguishable from one another. Furthermore, such actions and responses are fluctuant and variable in frequency, intensity, and consistency. Above all, the empathic attitude can only occur bilaterally.

Empathic elements in psychotherapy are inseparable from the intersubjective activity of therapy. We therapists must strive to avoid the concretization and objectification of our empathizing. Sometimes we empathize more profoundly than at other times, that is, we are in a more empathic mood. Yet, that is an intersubjective phenomenon, not a technical skill.

IS *VICARIOUS INTROSPECTION* AN INTERSUBJECTIVE PHENOMENON?

Vicarious introspection is a very important operational term introduced by Kohut (1977). It essentially indicates that, through empathy, the therapist self object can replicate and extend the patient's experience within his or her own mind. In this way the therapist's identification with the patient is intensified, resulting in an increased effective empathic understanding. Vicarious introspection is one way to describe an essential, invariable therapeutic process. It is important to remember, however, that this is an illusion, rather than an actuality of replication.

The term vicarious introspection deliberately maintains the focus on the patient's subjectivity, even as it refers to an event that seems mainly to involve the therapist's subjectivity. It is as though Kohut (1977), in order to legitimize inclusion of the therapist's subjective involvement in the therapeutic process, had to label it in such a way that it could be regarded as a derivative, subsidiary manifestation, however important, of the patient's subjective activity.

We have no violent objection to the term vicarious introspection. However, we prefer terms that acknowledge the complete co-equality of the therapist's subjectivity in the therapeutic situation; the term vicarious introspection lacks the explanatory element we seek. From beginning to end, the therapist's subjective life is an active part of the therapeutic process, and the therapist's subjectivity is initiating as well as reacting to the patient's subjective experience.

Vicarious derives from a word meaning substitution or change. Hence, the introspection that is vicarious is an altered experience, not quite the real thing. That is, the real thing occurs in the patient. To this we object. The subjective experience of each party is inseparable from that of the other. It does not acknowledge the full intersubjective reality to subordinate one set of subjective experience (the therapist's) to another (the patient's).

A therapist who is working well with his or her own subjectivity may regard and describe the experience as vicarious introspection. However, such an explanatory term does not fully acknowledge the role of the therapist's subjectivity.

IS THE CONCEPT OF *RESISTANCE*
COMPATIBLE WITH INTERSUBJECTIVE
THERAPY?

Resistance has always referred to an obstruction, interference, or complication of the therapeutic process. The term has been under attack from self psychologists because of their view that therapy will proceed effectively only if the therapist is sufficiently well attuned to be a suitable self object for the patient at this time and place. We applaud the self psychological emphasis on the therapist's responsibility, which is of extreme importance. When a therapist labels a patient as resisting, the therapist is often being defensive and lacks understanding of what the patient is attempting to co-create with the therapist. Yet, we prefer to retain the concept of resistance.

Even the self psychological argument against resisting can be turned in favor of resisting as follows. If we assume that things go wrong in therapy due to the limitations of the therapist (and not the patient), are we not assuming that there is some kind of resisting operating in the therapist? And, if the therapist, who is basically the same kind of human being as the patient, can have resistance, then why cannot the patient also have resistance?

The concept of resistance, or as Schafer (1976) would say, resisting, is valuable and heuristically powerful. It allows the therapist to grasp the self-protective aspects of the patient's behavior. This in turn leads to understanding of the patient's most profound fears over classic danger situations that were initially enunciated by Freud.

So we assume that both parties to therapy, the patient and the therapist, resist. We assume that each brings to the therapy his or her own idiosyncratic view of the universe. We could think of these views as the particular bundle of prejudices that each human being carries in life (Gadamer 1962). Part of the effect of these prejudices is to protect the patient from awareness of horrifying danger situations in the past. This is part of the historical dimension of subjectivity.

In order to develop and maintain my assemblage of prejudices, it is necessary for me to resist all the other prejudices that people carry.

In that respect, resistance is a generic phenomenon. It is a conserving and maintaining tendency, and it opposes all other beliefs. Resisting is thus a moral experience. That is, it helps maintain the true belief; it protects my view of the universe from invasion or alteration by yours.

In therapy, each party attempts to influence the other party to accept his or her view of the universe. This is not the only tendency, because each party also wishes to be changed in the direction of the other's world view. This view of therapy obviously is related to Hegel's (1807) master–slave dialectic and Husserl's (1950) master–disciple relationship [see Ricoeur (1986) on self psychology and phenomenological philosophy]. This represents a continuous and universally occurring form of resisting — normative resistance.

Yet, practically, we usually think of resistance when therapy seems blocked. We tend to think usually of the patient resisting, and the therapist counterresisting, or both. This is an important clinical discrimination to strive for. It tells us where to situate the therapeutic focus; the details of the manifest resistance must be established, whether in the patient, the therapist, or both. Yet, even if it seems quite clear that the resisting is primarily occurring in one of the parties, it should be remembered that this is a secondary phenomenon. Ultimately, this clinically familiar resistance will be traceable to the more fundamental resistance, whereby we maintain our basic prejudices and therefore attempt to immunize ourselves against change.

IS *CORRECTIVE EMOTIONAL EXPERIENCE* AN IMPORTANT PRECURSOR OF CLINICAL INTERSUBJECTIVITY?

The introduction of this term by Franz Alexander and Thomas French (1946) was one of the decisive post-Freudian events that led ultimately to the emergence of the intersubjective in psychoanalysis and psychotherapy. *Corrective emotional experience* is subversive in the best psychoanalytic sense. Just as Freud's introduction of psychoanalysis, with its emphasis on unconscious intentionality, subverted the conventions of the nineteenth and early twentieth centuries, so did Alexander and French's contribution undermine the prevailing psychoanalytic belief in the desirability and possibility of a neutral, objective, and detached analyst. These traditional psychoanalytic assumptions had made it feasible to believe in a unitary correct technique that, when learned, could be applied in all cases. If the analyst adhered consistently to correct technique, the treatment would succeed. If under these conditions, the treatment did not succeed, it was because the case was untreatable. Thus, a virtual universe of potentially significant variables could be ignored. The notion of psychotherapy as a corrective emotional experience was extremely discomfiting for those who found satisfaction in the psychoanalytic status quo because it meant thinking about the uniqueness of each patient-therapist match. This focus, in turn, necessarily implied variability, complexity, uncertainty, and ambiguity in every therapeutic pair.

Alexander and French believed that the therapist should discern the attitude required by the patient and that the adoption of this attitude by the therapist would establish the corrective emotional experience needed by the patient. It was probably the intersubjective potential of their concept that most threatened conservative analysts. Yet, the conservatives chose to focus their criticism on the element of deliberate, conscious manipulation. This element seems secondary to the more important focus on the unique, and not generalizable, need of the patient for a very special kind of experience.

This last consideration is essentially the same as our focus on the special view of the universe with which the patient meets the therapist. It seems likely, therefore, that Alexander and French intuitively, but perhaps not consciously, sensed that the therapist also brought an idiosyncratic world view to the therapeutic encounter and that it was the interplay of these two paradigms that generated the transformational process in therapy.

Corrective emotional experience is thus a very intersubjective term. Both patient and therapist partake of the
effects—both benefit, both are intensely involved emotionally and experientially. Hence, it is for both a corrective emotional experience and an intersubjective event.

DOES *ROLE RESPONSIVENESS* INDICATE AN INEVITABLE UNCONSCIOUS SUBJECTIVE RESPONSE OF THE THERAPIST?

Joseph Sandler (1976) introduced the term *role responsiveness* to indicate that the therapist, under optimal conditions, tends to assume a role that meets basic therapeutic
requirements of the patient. Sandler emphasizes that this
role assumption is not conscious and that the therapist
often becomes aware of his or her taking of this role only
as he or she is ready to relinquish it. Sandler noted that
this process of mutual enactment occurred constantly. He
coined the term *free-floating role responsiveness* to cap-
ture its ubiquity and place it on a par with free-floating
attention.

In this formulation, Sandler posits that the role
responsiveness is unconscious and is, of course, related to
the unconscious need that the patient has of the therapist.
However, he does not indicate the inseparability of role
response of the therapist from an unconscious need or
preoccupation of the therapist. The therapist's psychological needs had not yet become a focus of psychoanalytic

thinking. We now realize that the therapeutic response of the therapist has special, profound psychological importance to the therapist. So, in a sense, the role response of each party is meeting a need in himself or herself as well as in the other party. Thus, we can now have a clearly intersubjective perspective in the concept of role responsiveness.

DO *THERAPEUTIC ALLIANCE* AND *WORKING ALLIANCE* ANTICIPATE THE INTERSUBJECTIVE APPROACH?

Zetzel (1956) introduced the term *therapeutic alliance* and Greenson (1965) coined the term *working alliance*. These two concepts were intended to help account for the fact that a therapeutic relationship is motivated by a shared desire of the two participants. These concepts, like transitional phenomena, were regarded as both transferential (and countertransferential) and not transferential (and not countertransferential).

The authors attempted with these concepts to account for a shared attitude of therapeutic motivation. This joint state of mind partook of transference and countertransference, yet it needed to be preserved and strengthened — rather than analyzed away. The acknowledgment of jointness, of collaboration, of an intimate sharing hints strongly at an intersubjective experience.

Perhaps working alliance or therapeutic alliance is just another way of stating that a powerful intersubjective process develops in every productive therapeutic situation. It may well be that an examination of a therapeutic or working alliance would reveal the respective fantasies of patient and therapist that conjoin to create the alliance. In other words, the terms therapeutic alliance and working alliance are general descriptions, rather than specific definitions. The descriptions point to, but do not define, a very specific and meaning-laden intersubjective relationship.

The terms therapeutic alliance and working alliance are useful, but only if they are recognized as descriptive references to a dimension of intersubjectivity. The alliance reflects the feeling of power shared by the therapeutic participants as they jointly create new meanings through the interplay of their subjectivities.

If we view the alliances in this way, we can anticipate and accept fluctuations of the special experience of mutuality as the intersubjective process unfolds.

HOW DOES *ENACTMENT* EXEMPLIFY THE IRREDUCIBLE SUBJECTIVE INVOLVEMENT OF THE THERAPIST?

We confess to special fondness for the concept of *enactment*. Although it is obviously related to acting out, it does not possess the negative and pathological implications of that term. One might say that the term enactment is the inevitable outcome of the abolition of the strict division between thought and action that became so traditional in psychoanalysis.

Enactment, in its most current meaning, indicates

that, in the therapeutic situation, both patient and therapist are continuously living out in the relationship some fantasy of fundamental importance to each party. Such enactment does not occur sporadically or intermittently. Instead, it is a continuous phenomenon; it inheres in any human relationship. One might say, to relate is to enact.

Insight into enactment — that is, realizing that one is enacting and what the enactment means — will change the quantity and/or quality of enactment, but it will not eliminate enactment. Enactment is bilaterally continuous in a relationship.

Sometimes an enactment is blatant; sometimes an enactment is subtle. There is no escape. If a therapist resolves to prevent enactment by attempting to be detached, objective, neutral, or free of emotionality, he or she is now simply being defensive about the enactment, the occurrence of which is inevitable. When the therapist cannot recognize enactment by himself or herself, then he or she should search all the more assiduously for the presence and meaning of the enactment that is surely occurring.

The understanding of the mutual enactments and their interpenetration of both cause and effect provides enormous enrichment to the therapeutic experience.

Therefore, it seems obvious that, since enactment is inevitable, the therapist should not become engaged in a frenzied preoccupation with enactments and their meanings. Since much of the enactment arises from unconscious sources, the therapist is often unable to detect the presence, let alone the meaning, of an enactment until it has ripened and manifested itself repeatedly. A therapist's receptiveness to the occurrence of enactment and a corresponding willingness to view himself or herself in an enacting role will facilitate the realization that enactment is going on and what it means.

9

Representative Clinical Approaches to Intersubjectivity

Jacobs does not specifically define himself as an intersubjectivist, but we perceive important intersubjective qualities in his work, which we attempt to show in a discussion of his theoretical comments and his clinical demonstrations.

Jacobs (1993) states in regard to the interactive aspect of the psychoanalytic situation:

> Briefly summarized, this viewpoint stresses the following ideas: that the analytic process inevitably involves the

interplay of two psychologies, that the inner experiences of the analyst often provide a valuable pathway to understanding the inner experiences of the patient, and that not infrequently the analytic progress depends on the working through of resistance in the analyst as well as the patient. [p. 7]

In the above statement, Jacobs clearly emphasizes the importance of the analyst's continuing self-analysis, and he also makes a definite, but still ambiguous, reference to the intersubjective nature of the analytic process by saying that the "analytic process involves the interplay of two psychologies" (p. 7). Yet, Jacobs does not explain what he means by "involves." We hope to employ this ambiguous verb to show the nature of this involvement.

Jacobs (1993) presents one analytic session to illustrate his position. He accomplishes his task with grace and artistry. The presentation is rich, subtle, and witty. We return to the connotative importance of these qualities later.

The patient is a 38-year-old man who is an underachiever, has no friends, and cannot commit to a woman. Jacobs reports that he wonders if the patient is a charlatan, that he sometimes regards the patient as a menacing man with a possible streak of violence. He also feels that his space is being invaded by the patient.

Jacobs (1993) states, "My transference to Mr. V. has drawn much from my relationship to my father and other male authority figures" (p. 9). He perceives competitive and identificatory attitudes to the patient, and he regularly realizes how these feelings are connected to his life conflicts with his father. Throughout the session (and presumably the analysis) Jacobs relies on his own life history, and especially his relationship to his father.

For instance, he tells the reader that he cautioned himself to be alert for his own competitive feelings and for his chronic pattern of avoiding such feelings in order to sidestep any conflict with the father figure. In one example, he associates to his mortification over his father's rages, and he connects this with apprehensiveness over the patient's fury.

In various circumstances the analyst recognizes how closely his feelings and thoughts match those of his patient, and he correlates these reactions to his conflicted relationship to his father. The analyst is reliving important elements of his ambivalent relationship to his father as the hour unfolds. The intensity and authenticity of Jacobs's associative activity enliven and empower the analytic process. This associative activity is an important intersubjective activity, and it represents one dimension of the therapist's co-creative contribution. We might characterize it as an immediate or interactional aspect of intersubjectivity. We believe that Jacobs would agree with our view of his interactional impact on the analytic process, even though he does not explicitly give credit to his immediate subjective experience as a generative factor.

Yet, another intersubjective dimension also exists. This aspect is more controversial, and we do not know whether Jacobs would agree with it. Here we refer not to the emotional and associative state in the analyst that is activated by the patient, as described in the preceding paragraph. Rather, a lasting part of Jacobs's view of his world is his intense, ambivalent relationship to his father.

Jacobs brings this aspect of his life history to every significant intimate encounter. Thus, the patient's problems not only activated Jacobs's similar issues but also his conflicts activated those of the patient.

This kind of ever-present, continuous, reciprocally influencing state exists at all times in every analysis. That is, the analyst and the patient are initiating reactions in one another. During this process some degree of fusion of the two persons occurs, resulting in creative change in both.

We perceive in the witty, subtle quality of Jacobs's analytic dialogue with the patient a rich metacommunicative text. It is in that zone of communication that the initiating influence of the analyst upon the patient always occurs, whether or not it is evident in the manifest communication.

WHAT IS THOMAS OGDEN'S CLINICAL INTERSUBJECTIVE CONTRIBUTION?

Ogden (1994) postulates the "analytic third" (p. 4). This is the intersubjective state jointly created by patient and analyst, and it exists in continuous dialectical tension with the separate subjectivities of both patient and analyst.

Ogden describes how the analytic third developed in two cases and how its occurrence was crucial for productive further unfolding of the analysis.

The first case involves a middle-aged man who suffers "extreme emotional detachment from both himself and from other people" (p. 5). Ogden provides abundant details of the patient's analytic behavior to support this view of the patient. Ogden (1994) told the patient that the patient's associations to bankruptcy, exhaustion, and a near-fatal accident represented an "inchoate" feeling that the treatment was diminished, empty, moribund. The patient was having rudimentary feelings that he and the analyst were not conversing in a way that seemed alive. Instead, the analyst seemed to the patient to have to be mechanical with him, just as the patient could not be human with the analyst.

Ogden then reports that he became aware of the huge effort that he and the patient regularly exerted to prevent the analysis from "collapsing into despair." Ogden had the fantasy of the two of them in the past trying frantically to maintain a beach ball in the air, hitting it to one another.

From his side, Ogden reports that during this same session he was having associations to his own current life that involved acute disappointment, feelings of being duped by a false intimation of specialness, "narcissistic" (p. 6) professional thoughts, and someone slamming a door in his face — producing a profound, intense feeling of desolation and isolation. Later, Ogden notes that he was becoming able to describe for himself the desperate feeling he had been having as he and the patient searched frantically for personal and human elements in their analytic work. Ogden also started to feel that he comprehended some pain, anger, and despair that were associated with the experience of colliding repeatedly with an object that looks human but feels mechanical and impersonal.

The preceding comments convey the sense of Ogden's meaning of the analytic third. Ogden (1994) states that after his painful inner experiences, "I was more receptive to the schizoid quality of his [the patient's] experience and to the hollowness of both his and my own attempts to create something together that felt real" (p. 9). Ogden believes that the analytic third stimulated in him the harrowing subjective experiences he endured in the session, for he writes, "The fantasy involving [the slamming of the door in his face] was created at that moment not by me in isolation, but through my participation in the intersubjective experience with [the patient]" (p. 10).

Ogden (1994) presents a second case about which he states, "My own and the patient's capacity to think as separate individuals had been co-opted by the intensity of the shared unconscious fantasy/somatic delusion in which we were both enmeshed" (p. 15). This portrays another aspect of the analytic third as Ogden perceives it.

Ogden writes further that "the experience of the third (although jointly created) is not identical for each participant. Moreover, the analytic third is an asymmetrical construction because it is generated in a context of the analytic setting which is powerfully defined by the relationship of roles of analyst and analysand. Therefore, Ogden writes, the unconscious experience of the patient is privileged in a special way, in that the present and past experience of the patient is assumed by the analytic pair to be the primary (but not exclusive) subject of the analytic dialogue. He adds that the analyst's experience as a part of the analytic third is mainly used as a vehicle for understanding the analysand's conscious and unconscious experience. And Ogden notes parenthetically that "the analyst and analysand are not engaged in a democratic process of mutual analysis" (p. 17).

We do not take serious issue with this last statement

of Ogden's. We also do not recommend mutual analysis and agree that the patient's life is the major subject of the therapeutic discourse. The asymmetry of therapy is a basic necessity. The roles of therapist and patient are quite different. And yet, at another level, in another way — that may always remain invisible and inaudible — there is a condition of co-equality, of co-creativeness that encompasses the entire therapeutic experience, permeating and influencing the asymmetrical conditions, even as it does not abolish them.

This is a messier formulation than the notion of the analytic third, which presupposes three distinct categories of analytic subjectivity. Yet, our suggestion has the surpassing virtue of affirming the inchoate nature of the therapeutic experience and thus maintaining an heuristically valuable attitude.

It is not clear from Ogden's report whether he credits the analyst's involvement in the analytic third with an initiating or only a reactive role. His case material is used only to illustrate the analyst's receptive and reactive role. We, of course, believe that the therapist co-creates the unconscious phenomena along with the patient. From his report, it seems that Ogden may still be unsure about this matter.

WHAT IS THE DISCLOSURE-ENACTMENT-INTERPRETIVE METHOD OF DAVIES?

Davies (1994) recently published a very interesting report of a case in which she disclosed her sexual feelings toward a male patient. Although such disclosure is traditionally regarded unfavorably, we wish to focus on its therapeutic meaning and implications.

Davies subscribes to a "relational two-person model" (p. 167) of psychoanalysis. She believes that psychic meaning does not exist solely within the patient. Rather, she conceives of a "mutually constructed, intersubjective playground of transitional potentialities where meaning can be constructed only in the throes of recognition, destruction, and perpetual interaction between two actively engaged participants" (p. 168). In such a climate, meanings that seem dangerous to either party can be repressed by either one. Davies further states that when the patient is terrified of a subject matter, the analyst must

> recognize and maintain such disavowed experiences until such time as the patient can know them and integrate them without the threatening perception of debilitating anxiety and psychic regression. Within such a scenario, the analyst oftentimes must speak the dangerously charged words for the first time. [p. 168]

She reports the case of a young mathematician with rich, erotic fantasies toward women. Whenever he tried to talk to a woman, however, he became panicky and developed what he called a "rather urgent and threatening nausea" (p. 162). If approached seductively by a woman, he would reject her coldly.

Davies found it somewhat surprising that the patient began reporting very eroticized feelings to her. He described intense sexual fantasies and idealized her as the only person who could release him from his sexual prison.

Davies reports that she enjoyed his ardent associations. She was shocked to become aware that she envied the woman who would become his future lover, and she re-experienced "grandiose oedipal desires. . . .Clearly, I had left the real world behind and had entered with my patient a shared illusion of oedipal passion, victory, and remorse, as much a subject of my own resurrected struggle, as I have become the object of his" (p. 163).

Perhaps one of the reasons Davies could not respond interpretively was because, as soon as the patient sensed her readiness to speak about the erotic sensuality, he took steps to foreclose her action. She notes that the patient's persona and attitude changed at the very moment that she was going to intervene. She writes that at the precise moment that she was about to "step inside and become a more active participant" (pp. 163–164) in the process between them he would seem to "implode upon himself" (pp. 163–164), would sink into his chair, his voice would become whining and grating, as though he had no right to his feelings about the analyst. He pictured the analyst as laughing at him and derogating him to her friends.

Davies reports that at these moments her feelings of warmth and arousal would dissolve immediately and instead she would feel misled, seduced, and infuriated. She also became aware of abdominal feelings of nausea. At this juncture, Davies reports recognizing her feelings as a "road map" (p. 164) to his subjectivity. She shies away from a fuller intersubjective analysis by not fully exploring, or at least sharing, that explanation with us. We do not know whether she did it on her own, why she felt so enraged, and what further feelings were stirred up in her

by the patient's actions. What was the content of her
subjectivity? What story of love, surprise, rejection, or
vengeance had she co-created with Mr. M.?

We assume that Davies offered no interpretation to
the patient because she believed he was not ready and that
it remained her role to know this aspect of his subjectivity
and to hold onto it until such time as he would allow her
to talk about it without feeling overwhelmed. Another
possibility is that *she* was not ready to discuss the matter
for reasons stemming from the pain created with Mr. M.
relating to her current or past life. Perhaps the intensity of
the letdown she experienced left her speechless and ignited
unresolved issues from her life.

Davies tells us that eventually the time came when the
patient needed to confront her as a sexual person. In other
words, she judged him ready to put his erotic stories
together with his sense of her as a real sexual woman — not
one who was going to get sick of him, withdraw, or cause
him to flee.

The clinical problem throughout the analysis was
that, just as his mother had conveyed the impression that
sexuality was disgusting, so would all women toward
whom he felt desire. So, he felt, would be Davies's feelings
toward him.

In fact, we know Mr. M. did not consciously realize
the impact of his behavior because Davies next tells us of
her attempts to lead Mr. M. to see that possibly his mother
had felt revulsion over her own sexual feelings toward her
little son. Perhaps in this intimate period she became so
highly aroused, even exceeding her denial threshold. Mr.

M. became enraged at these ideas and announced that mothers no more have such feelings toward their children than analysts do toward their patients.

Davies, at this juncture, believed that she had to confront the patient with his denial of her and his mother's sexuality. The path she wanted to choose was open confrontation. In other words, she wanted to tell him directly that she was sexual in regard to him and that he was denying it. As she pondered this confrontation, she at first felt guilty. Yet, then she decided that she was placing allegiance to what she describes as "an impersonal theory" (p. 163) ahead of clinical necessity. The theory she refers to supposedly taught that sexual countertransference should be worked through alone, not shared with the patient. Such analyzed countertransference could enhance the analyst's understanding of the patient, but sharing such countertransference with the patient would be tantamount to committing sexual incest. Implied is her belief that others felt that to enter into an enactment of "symbolic incest" (p. 165) would be so inappropriate that it would ruin the analysis. In contrast, the reliance on such stereotypes and maintaining the appearance of neutrality would actually be a sadistic gratification of the patient's basically masochistic beliefs about the nature of his relationship with women—including the analyst.

Davies decided to break the logjam and share the presence of her sexual feelings with Mr. M. She did so after working through her fear of becoming an "overwhelming, pre-oedipal, chasmic mother" (p. 166) for the patient. She also worked through her anxiety over reliving intense, intrusive memories of being enmeshed erotically, as well as the fear of reexperiencing the struggle to overcome idealized oedipal romantic fantasies.

Finally one day, Davies tells Mr. M. that she often has had sexual fantasies about him, at times during the sessions and also when she was alone. She adds that they are not going to act on them, but that she could think of no other way to counter his denial that a woman, especially his mother, might have felt that way.

The patient's immediate reaction was one of intense rage and shock. He charged her with criminality in the form of malpractice and perversion, and muttered that she nauseated him and that he felt like he was going to vomit.

Davies counters by saying there is nothing sick and disgusting about her or his sexual feelings. She tells him this is how he felt when his mother withdrew from him. She also alluded to his guilty fear of punishment by a father figure.

Mr. M.'s initial rage was only momentary shock. He did not disorganize. The analysis was not derailed. Instead, the work intensified and progressed satisfactorily. The patient commented on the beauty of the oedipal object. Davies emphasized that women are responsible for their sexual desires. "The patient began to weep, he punched his fist into his palm repeatedly" (p. 166). She told him that she thought he was just furious that he had been forced by his mother's attitudes to feel shame over both their sexual feelings. Davies pointed out that his mother was revolted and disgusted by her sexual feelings toward the patient, that she had much shame, and that she made him believe the shame rested solely on him. At a later time, Davies deepened the interpretation by bringing it into their relationship, noting that perhaps he resented the analyst for permitting him to shoulder all the responsibility for all the erotic feelings in the analysis.

Davies waited a long time before confronting Mr. M. She intuitively felt he was ready. Before confronting him, she herself felt agonized and scared of doing something wrong. It seems that patient and analyst mutually constructed a state of being in which they were like two prepubescent children groping toward sexual talk. Who would break the ice first? Sometimes the analyst has to; sometimes it is important for the patient to do so. Most of the time it probably does not make any difference, and whichever way the pair chooses, there is some fallout that needs to be analyzed.

Our view of therapy is one in which we see both parties so intimately involved over time that eventually their significant feelings are transparent to one another. Many theoretical models attempt to deny this transparency and end up talmudically pondering such questions as whether or not to reveal significant affective states to patients. It is improbable that by telling Mr. M. that she had sexual feelings, Davies was saying something that he did not already unconsciously know. Like two young children intensely wrapped up with one another, each one knew the other knew about the other's sexuality. The main issue for Davies remained how to tell the patient when she decided to do so. The meaning of making overt what they both knew is also of paramount importance for the analyst to ponder.

Finally, we wish to draw attention to the enactment

that accompanies the interpretation. Davies acknowledges that the enactment represents some consummation and gratification of incestuous desires. She, in fact, argues that it is important for this patient not simply to renounce his oedipal desires as if the parent had none of her own. She argues

> It is only when such erotically-charged material can be spoken of, that it can be changed, modified, withdrawn, renewed, when it can become the substance of all forms of symbolic and illusory play; that the patient can both "have" and "not have" . . . the experience of oedipal success. [p. 169]

Davies believes that in such a climate, the patient can "revel" in states of oedipal potency and desire and that the analytic frame offers safety from transgression of the incest barrier. In other words, Davies is positing that the patient can learn to enjoy sensuous sexual desires and must not simply renounce them. She adds that she believes that when patient and analyst negotiate successfully this paradox of development, a basis is established that will enable the patient eventually to mourn successfully that which cannot be, while maintaining an effective hope in all that is possible.

Davies's pivotal disclosure-enactment-interpretation accomplished one of the functions of an enactment that Renik (1993) has pointed to as critical. It allowed a spontaneous corrective emotional experience to occur. The patient was thrust into a world where healthy sexual play between mother and child was not just allowed, but needed for development without breaking the incest barrier. Now growth through play and through mourning could be accomplished. The patient's mother blocked that growth. The analyst corrected that humiliating emotional experience. The enactment allowed the vital emotional corrective experience. The awkwardness of the interpretive process allowed the enactment. And finally, intersubjective immersion in which the subjectivity of the analyst was given co-equality with that of patient gave birth to that inelegant, awkward, but deeply effective interpretation.

References

Alexander, F., and French, T. (1946). *Psychoanalytic Therapy*. New York: Ronald.

Aron, L. (1991a). The patient's experience of the analyst's subjectivity. *Psychoanalytic Dialogues* 1:29–51.

_____ (1991b). One person and two person psychologies and the method of psychoanalysis. *Psychoanalytic Psychology* 7:475–485.

_____ (1992). From Ferenczi to Searles and contemporary relational approaches: (Commentary on Mark Blechner's "Working in the Countertransference." *Psychoanalytic Dialogues* 2:181–190.

Atwood, G. E. and Stolorow, R. D. (1984). *Structures of Subjectivity: Explorations in Psychoanalytic Phenomenology*. Hillsdale, NJ: Analytic Press.

Beebe, B., and Lachmann, F. (1988a). The contribution of mother–infant mutuality to the origins of self and object representations. *Psychoanalytic Psychology* 5:305–337.

_____ (1988b). Mother–infant mutual influence and precursors of psychic structure. In *Frontiers in Self Psychology: Progress in Self Psychology, Vol. 4*, ed. A. Goldberg, pp. 3–25. Hillsdale: NJ: Analytic Press.

Benjamin, J. (1988). *The Bonds of Love: Psychoanalysis, Feminism, and the Problem of Domination.* New York: Pantheon.

——— (1992). Recognition and destruction: an outline of intersubjectivity. In *Relational Perspectives in Psychoanalysis*, ed. N. J. Skolnick, and S. C. Warshaw, pp. 43–60. Hillsdale, NJ: Analytic Press.

Davies, J. (1994). Love in the afternoon: a relational consideration of desire and dread in the countertransference. *Psychoanalytic Dialogues* 4(2):153–170.

Epstein, L., and Feiner, A. (1979). *Countertransference: The Therapist's Contribution to the Therapeutic Situation.* New York: Jason Aronson.

Ferenczi, S. (1988). *The Clinical Diary of Sandor Ferenczi.* Trans. J. Dupont. Cambridge, MA: Harvard University Press.

Freud, S. (1912). Recommendations to physicians practicing psychoanalysis. *Standard Edition* 12:109–120.

Gadamer, H-G. (1962). On the problem of self-understanding. In *Philosophical Hermeneutics*, trans. and ed. D. E. Linge, pp. 44–58. Berkeley, CA: University of California Press, 1976.

——— (1966). The universality of the hermeneutical problem. In *Philosophical Hermeneutics*, trans. and ed. D. E. Linge, pp. 3–17. Berkeley, CA: University of California Press, 1976.

——— (1967). On the scope and function of hermeneutical reflection, trans. G. B. Hess and R. E. Palmer. In *Philosophical Hermeneutics*, trans. and ed. D. E. Linge, pp. 18–43. Berkeley, CA: University of California Press, 1976.

——— (1975). *Truth and Method*, trans. and ed. G. Barden and J. Cumming. New York: Seabury Press, 1960.

Gill, M. M. (1982). *Analysis of Transference I: Theory and Technique.* New York: International Universities Press.

Gill, M. M. and Hoffman, I. Z. (1982). *Analysis of Transference II: Studies of Nine Audio Recorded Psychoanalytic Sessions.* New York: International Universities Press.

Greenson, R. (1965). The working alliance and the transference neurosis. *Psychoanalytic Quarterly* 34:155–181.

Hegel, G. W. F. (1807). *Phenomenology of Spirit*, trans. A. V. Miller. Oxford: Clarendon, 1977.

Hoffman, I. Z. (1983). The patient as interpreter of the analyst's experience. *Contemporary Psychoanalysis* 19(3):389–422.

——— (1991a). Discussion: toward a social-constructivist view of the psychoanalytic situation. *Psychoanalytic Dialogues* 1:74–105.

——— (1991b). Reply to Benjamin. *Psychoanalytic Dialogues* 1:535–544.

——— (1992). Some practical implications of a social-constructivist view of the psychoanalytic situation. *Psychoanalytic Dialogues* 2(3):287–304.

Horney, K. (1939). *New Ways in Psychoanalysis.* New York: Norton.

Husserl, E. (1950). *Cartesian Meditations: An Introduction to Phenomenology*, trans. D. Cairns. The Hague: Martinus Nijhoff, 1964.

Isakower, O. (1957–1963). *Unpublished minutes of curriculum committee and faculty meetings*. New York: New York Psychoanalytic Institute.

Jacobs, T. (1991). *The Use of the Self*. Madison, CT: International Universities Press.

_____ (1993). The inner experiences of the analyst: their contribution to the analytic process. *International Journal of Psycho-Analysis* 74:7–14.

Klein, G. S. (1976). *Psychoanalytic Theory: An Exploration of Essentials*. New York: International Universities Press.

Kohut, H. (1977). *The Restoration of the Self*. New York: International Universities Press.

Lear, J. (1990). *Love and Its Place in Nature*. New York: Farrar, Straus, and Giroux.

Lichtenberg, J. (1983). *Psychoanalysis and Infant Research*. Hillsdale, NJ: Analytic Press.

_____ (1989). *Psychoanalysis and Motivation*. Hillsdale, NJ: Analytic Press.

Lipton, S. D. (1977a). The advantages of Freud's technique as shown in his analysis of the rat man. *International Journal of Psycho-Analysis* 58:255–273.

_____ (1977b). Clinical observations on resistance to the transference. *International Journal of Psycho-Analysis* 58:463–472.

Loewald, H. (1960). On the therapeutic action of psychoanalysis. *International Journal of Psycho-Analysis* 41:16–33.

Macalpine, I. (1950). The development of the transference. *Psychoanalytic Quarterly* 19:501–539.

McLaughlin, J. (1981). Transference, psychic reality and countertransference. *Psychoanalytic Quarterly* 50:639–664.

Natterson, J. (1991). *Beyond Countertransference: The Therapist's Subjectivity in the Therapeutic Process*. Northvale, NJ: Jason Aronson.

Ogden, T. H. (1994). The analytic third: working with intersubjective clinical facts. *International Journal of Psycho-Analysis* 75:3–19.

Poland, W. (1986). The analyst's words. *Psychoanalytic Quarterly* 57:244–271.

_____ (1988). Insight and the analytic dyad. *Psychoanalytic Quarterly* 57:341–370.

Racker, H. (1968). *Transference and Countertransference*. New York: International Universities Press.

Renik, O. (1993a). Countertransference enactment and the psychoanalytic process. In *Psychic Structure and Psychic Change, Essays in Honor of Robert Wallerstein, M. D.*, ed. M. J. Horowitz, O. F. Kernberg, and E. M. Weinshel, pp. 135–158. Madison, CT: International Universities Press.

_____ (1993b). Analytic interaction: conceptualizing technique in light of the analyst's irreducible subjectivity. *Psychoanalytic Quarterly* 62:553-571.

Ricoeur, P. (1986). The self in psychoanalysis and in phenomenological philosophy. *Psychoanalytic Inquiry* 6(3): 437-458.

Sandler, J. (1976). Countertransference and role-responsiveness. *International Review of Psycho-Analysis* 3:43-47.

_____ (1983). Reflections on some relations between psychoanalytic concepts and psychoanalytic practice. *International Journal of Psycho-Analysis* 64:35-45.

Schafer, R. (1976). *A New Language for Psychoanalysis*. New Haven: Yale University Press.

_____ (1983). *The Analytic Attitude*. New York: Basic Books.

_____ (1992). *Retelling a Life: Dialogue and Narration in Psychoanalysis*. New York: Basic Books.

Schwaber, E. (1981). Empathy: a mode of psychoanalytic listening. *Psychoanalytic Inquiry* 1:357-392.

_____ (1983). Psychoanalytic listening and psychic reality. *International Review of Psycho-Analysis* 10:379-392.

Searles, H. (1975). *Countertransference and Related Subjects*. New York: International Universities Press.

Stern, D. (1985). *The Interpersonal World of the Infant*. New York: Basic Books.

Stern, D. B. (1991). A philosophy for the embedded analyst: Gadamer's hermeneutics and the social paradigm of psychoanalysis. *Contemporary Psychoanalysis* 27(1):51-79.

Stolorow, R. D., and Atwood, G. E. (1992). *Contexts of Being, The Intersubjective Foundations of Psychological Life*. Hillsdale, NJ: Analytic Press.

Stolorow, R. D., Atwood, G. E., and Brandchaft, B. (1994). *The Intersubjective Perspective*. Northvale, NJ: Jason Aronson.

Stolorow, R. D., Brandchaft, B., and Atwood, G. E. (1987). *Psychoanalytic Treatment: An Intersubjective Approach*. Hillsdale, NJ: Analytic Press.

Tansey, M., and Burke, W. (1989). *Understanding Countertransference: From Projective Identification to Empathy*. Hillsdale, NJ: Analytic Press.

Waelder, R. (1956). Introduction to the discussion on problems of transference. *International Journal of Psycho-Analysis* 37:367-370.

Winnicott, D. W. (1947). Hate in the countertransference. In *Through Paediatrics to Psychoanalysis*, pp. 194-203. New York: Basic Books, 1975.

_____ (1951). Transitional objects and transitional phenomena. In *Playing and Reality*, pp. 1-25. New York: Basic Books, 1971.

Wolstein, B. (1983). The pluralism of perspectives on countertransference. *Contemporary Psychoanalysis* 19:506–521.

_____ (1988). Introduction. In *Essential Papers on Countertransference*, ed. B. Wolstein, pp. 1–15. New York: New York University Press.

_____ (1994). The evolving newness of interpersonal psychoanalysis: from the vantage point of immediate experience. *Contemporary Psychoanalysis* 30:473–499.

Zetzel, E. (1956). Current concepts of transference. *International Journal of Psycho-Analysis* 37:369–376.

Index